50
WAYS
TO
TEACH
YOUR LEARNER

50 WAYS TO TEACH YOUR LEARNER

Activities and Interventions for Building High-Performance Teams

ED ROSE

WITH STEVE BUCKLEY

Jossey-Bass
Pfeiffer
San Francisco

Copyright © 1999 by Jossey-Bass/Pfeiffer

ISBN: 0-7879-4504-8

Library of Congress Cataloging-in-Publication Data

Rose, Ed (Edwin)

    50 ways to teach your learner : activities and interventions
for building high-performance teams / Ed Rose with Steve Buckley.
      p.   cm.
    ISBN 0-7879-4504-8 (acid-free paper)
    1. Teams in the workplace—Training of.   2. Experiential learning.
  I. Buckley, Steve, 1960–   II. Title   III. Title: Fifty ways to teach your learner
    HD66.R65   1998
    658.3'124—dc21   98-40206

Printed in the United States of America

Published by

Jossey-Bass Pfeiffer
350 Sansome Street, 5th Floor
San Francisco, California 94104-1342
(415) 433-1740; Fax (415) 433-0499
(800) 274-4434; Fax (800) 569-0443

Visit our website at: www.pfeiffer.com

Acquiring Editor: *Matthew Holt*

Director of Development: *Kathleen Dolan Davies*

Development Editor: *Susan Rachmeler*

Senior Production Editor: *Pamela Berkman*

Manufacturing Supervisor: *Becky Carreño*

Interior Designer: *Bruce Lundquist*

Cover Design: *Laurie Anderson*

Printing 10 9 8 7 6 5 4 3 2

 This book is printed on acid-free, recycled stock that meets or exceeds the minimum GPO and EPA requirements for recycled paper.

CONTENTS

Foreword   ix
Preface   xiii
Acknowledgments   xv
About the Authors   xvii

Part One: How to Use the Initiatives   3

Chapter One: Introduction to Experiential Learning   5

Chapter Two: Techniques for Facilitating Experiential Learning   9
The Harvest   9
The Facilitation Process   10
The Debriefing   12

Chapter Three: How to Use Initiatives   15

Part Two: The Initiatives   19

Adaptable: Initiatives that highlight communication, planning, and group dynamics
1. Silent Planning   21
   Focus: Communication systems
2. A Common Vision   23
   Focus: Teamwork, effective communication, problem solving
3. Noah's Ark   25
   Focus: Communication, planning, teamwork
4. Squares and More Squares   29
   Focus: Intra-team communication, planning, understanding the goal, benchmarking
5. Canyon of No Return   41
   Focus: Communication, building trust, physical constraints, leadership, teamwork
6. Space Station Lockout   47
   Focus: Problem solving, cooperation, communication
7. Human Web   53
   Focus: Getting to know others, warm up, problem solving, individual contributions to team activities
8. Team Power   57
   Focus: Teamwork, communication, problem solving
9. Yellow Gooey Sticky Mess   59
   Focus: Change and its effect on organizations, individuals and teams, organizational transformation

Trustworthy: Initiatives that highlight trust and mutual respect
10. Trust Walk   65
    Focus: Building trust, communication
11. Trust Me   67
    Focus: Building trust

12. The Sword in the Stone Team Challenge   69
    Focus: Team building, dynamic teamwork, appreciation of others, team problem solving
13. Willow Tree   77
    Focus: Supporting others, warm up, trust
14. How Many Balls Can You Juggle?   79
    Focus: Continuous improvement, interpersonal interaction, synergy, teamwork, customer/supplier relationships

Resourceful: Initiatives that highlight creativity, innovation, paradigms, breakthrough thinking, and problem solving

15. Breakthrough Thinking   81
    Focus: Breakthrough thinking, creativity, flexibility
16. The Acme Mining Company   85
    Focus: Manager/worker relationships, traditional management practices
17. Hunt for the Key Word   91
    Focus: Problem solving, creativity, breakthrough thinking
18. Which Hole Should I Work On?   101
    Focus: Spontaneous thinking, creativity, teamwork
19. Paper Bag   105
    Focus: Creativity, problem solving, design
20. State-of-the-Art Delivery System   109
    Focus: Creativity, teamwork, group dynamics, role clarification
21. Space Antenna   117
    Focus: Creativity, teamwork, group dynamics, role clarification
22. Mountain Lion and Rabbit   127
    Focus: Warm up, problem solving, working together, lateral thinking, creativity
23. The Swamp   131
    Focus: Teamwork, problem solving, collaboration
24. High Tide Islands and Jaws   135
    Focus: Teamwork, communication, problem solving
25. Does Your Mind Always Work?   137
    Focus: Creativity, problem solving, warm up
26. The Problem   139
    Focus: Creativity, problem solving
27. I'll Know It when I See It   143
    Focus: Approaches to problem solving, the value of information
28. Did You Say "Aircraft"?   147
    Focus: Thinking out-of-the-box, creativity
29. Making the News   151
    Focus: Intra-team communication, creativity, utilizing skills
30. Blind Puzzle   155
    Focus: Teamwork, problem solving, creativity
31. Wing It   159
    Focus: Teamwork, creativity, continuous improvement, warm up

Optimistic: Initiatives that highlight moving beyond perceived limits, challenging biases, managing conflict, and benchmarking

32. Workplace for Empowerment   163
    Focus: Workplace change, similarities among team members
33. World's Best Product   165
    Focus: Teamwork, synergy, interrelationships
34. Puzzel   167
    Focus: Breaking down perceived walls, benchmarking, communication
35. Dr. Rose vs. Dr. Buckley   177
    Focus: Conflict resolution

Considerate: Initiatives that highlight creativity, valuing diversity, cooperation, and collaboration

36. Save the Bucket   181
    Focus: Creativity, innovation
37. Team Walk   185
    Focus: Synergy, cooperation, teamwork
38. Research Team   189
    Focus: Teamwork in large groups, conflict resolution, negotiation, complex problem solving, collaboration
39. Spy Story   199
    Focus: Teamwork, cooperation, creativity, collaboration
40. Operation PVC   213
    Focus: Teamwork, out-of-the-box thinking, creativity
41. Hula Hoops   219
    Focus: Teamwork, breakthrough thinking, communication, planning
42. ATROC   221
    Focus: Team synergy, breaking down invisible walls, benchmarking, creativity, lateral thinking
43. Hearts Wars   227
    Focus: Teamwork, leadership, team dynamics, negotiation
44. Recognizing Each Team Member   231
    Focus: Ending sessions, recognizing one another for contributions

Debrief and Warm Up: Initiatives that prepare participants for upcoming events

45. Three Warm-Up Activities (Sharing, A Simple Task, and Understanding Emotions)   233
    Focus: Beginning a session, preparing for the day
46. Tag! You're It!   237
    Focus: Warm up, fun
47. The Blindfold Squares   241
    Focus: Warm up, communication, performing under pressure
48. Creative Balloons   243
    Focus: Warm up, fun, working together, creativity
49. The Final Debriefing   245
    Focus: Tie workshop together
50. It's All in Your Vision   247
    Focus: Vision, power of the mind

Appendix   249

DEDICATION

This book is dedicated to the manufacturing management team at Harris Semiconductor's, Palm Bay, Florida, site. Special recognition is deserved by Ray Odom and Steve Titus, who championed the transition to self-directed work teams, which required a large investment in training that they were willing to make. Their leadership and willingness to take a chance ultimately produced this book.

In addition to Ray and Steve, the rest of the Palm Bay leadership team deserves mention for their support of the process throughout the organization. They are:

Charlie Burns
Cindy Drapcho
Steve Gilmore
George Higgins
Brian Hagerty
Susan Jones
Jim Laibl
Jim McEllis
Steve Suhling
Bill Smoak
Gordon Taylor
Brian Weir

Here's to a great team! Your commitment to employee development has made this book possible.

FOREWORD

COMPETITIVENESS

The survival of business organizations is becoming more difficult. Globalization, the increasing rate of change, increasingly critical customers, and a changing work force are creating conditions that require businesses to become smarter and more flexible (Pinchot & Pinchot, 1996). These "smarter" organizations depend on employees who learn and an organizational infrastructure that promotes that learning. Training and development (T&D) departments have typically had the primary responsibility for providing formal learning opportunities within organizations. The "smartest" T&D departments have also become smarter; the perspective they bring to the problem of learning and the tools that fit that perspective have evolved to take into account the fact that the learners involved in those opportunities are adults.

WHAT IS LEARNING?

Learning involves the acquisition of knowledge, skills, and attitudes. Learning occurs in a wide array of situations; it may occur while a person is alone or with others, be intentional or unintentional, desired or undesired, formal or informal, textbook-based or experience-based. Learning can be viewed as a product or end result or as a process or means for obtaining a desired outcome. Learning is a necessary component of life, and the value and benefits of any learning opportunity can be enhanced, given the right conditions.

ADULT LEARNING

Adult learning theory was developed by Malcolm Knowles (1992) to provide insight into the way that adults learn. Knowles said that (1) adults are self-directed and therefore prefer to have some control over the learning situation; (2) adults bring their own unique experiences to the learning situation, which can serve as valuable resources; (3) adults' readiness to learn is most often determined by their current needs; and (4) because adults want to be able to apply tomorrow what they have learned today, emphasis should be placed on the practical application of the skills and knowledge obtained in the learning situation.

EXPERIENTIAL LEARNING

Experiential learning utilizes the principles set forth in adult learning theory to ensure maximum benefit for adults: (1) A problem-centered focus is used so that it is obvious to participants how the knowledge, skills, and abilities that are learned can be used on the job; (2) Active participant involvement is required, which allows the participants to control and enjoy their learning environment; (3) participants' varied experiences are incorporated, shared, and built upon; (4) active or "hands-on" learning through doing and discovery is emphasized. Research has shown that such "active learning" results in much higher information retention than other teaching or training methods (O'Neil, 1996).

TEAM LEARNING

Experiential activities are most effective when they are completed by whole teams in need of a specific type of training. The theory of situational learning and situational knowledge shows that the context in which learning takes place is critical for developing fuller understanding (Brown, Collins, & Duguid, 1989). Teams provide a social, psychological, and task context in which the employee works. Transfer of the learning to the workplace is also enhanced by training intact teams, as team members can help one another practice the new competencies by modeling, coaching, reinforcing, and understanding the new behaviors. The team thus becomes a microcosm of the learning organization.

USING THE ACTIVITIES

The activities in this book were crafted over a number of years and a number of training sessions with a variety of employees. That crafting increased their potential for value. Of course, *the potential value of any activity depends on timing and execution.* Value is higher if the team is ready for the lessons being taught, that is, when the activity is in response to a problem the team is experiencing *now,* which is the essence of just-in-time training. How much value is obtained depends on the facilitator as much as on the actual activity. Facilitators must be prepared, manage the learning environment and the learning process, and debrief properly to enhance and cement the learnings.

FACILITATION OF LEARNING

People have different levels of learning ability and different skills, depending on topic or circumstances. None of us is a great learner in every situation. All of us can use the aid of an expert facilitator in some situations.

Facilitators of experiential activities have developed the skills needed to organize, supervise, and debrief the learning activities, to understand the dynamics of groups, and to handle interpersonal conflict that may arise.

NONTHREATENING ENVIRONMENT

A nonthreatening environment is essential for learning to occur during a training program. Participants may feel at risk because of the changes expected of them. This feeling often results in discomfort and resistance to change. Therefore, the learning environment should be as pleasant, comfortable, and nonthreatening as the achievement of learning goals will allow. An environment that is conducive to change can be created through application of the principles of adult learning, such as treating adults as responsible individuals and allowing them some control over the learning environment.

TRANSFER OF LEARNING TO THE JOB

A major criticism of classroom training has been that what is learned is often not transferred back to the job. Data suggests that few traditional classroom lessons are ever demonstrated on the job when participants go back to work. Studies have shown that the learning environment should be as similar to the job environment as possible to maximize transfer. Training intact teams is one way to provide a similar environment. Training that is obviously related to current problems the team is facing also increases transfer. Debriefing also enhances team members' abilities to talk about what they have learned after returning to the job, which can help them to review, practice, and reinforce their learnings back on the job. Experiential learning enables participants to learn through multiple channels: hearing, seeing, and experiencing the lessons personally, which enhances recall.

TRAINING EVALUATION

Training programs must be evaluated to ensure that they are as effective and successful as possible and that their benefits outweigh their costs. Such evaluation increasingly is becoming a strategic necessity, what with internal competition for scarce training resources.

Knowles (1992) recommends Kirkpatrick's (1972) four-level model for evaluation as most congruent with an adult learning approach. Kirkpatrick's four levels are *reaction, learning, behavior,* and *results.* Participants' reactions to a training program provide valuable feedback, but what was actually learned must be assessed. Changes in behavior on the job must be measured and, finally, the organizational results that can be attributed to the training program should be assessed.

CONCLUSION

Learning by employees at all levels in a business produces value in the form of intellectual capital (Purser & Montuori, 1995). Managers are starting to think about intellectual resources of the business as well as financial capital and facilities, and social, human, and organizational capital. Experiential approaches to learning that involve intact teams have been shown to be a quick, effective way to build that intellectual capital. The benefits certainly outweigh the costs. The activities and approach described in this book, when used within the context of adult learning theory, will generate valuable learning opportunities for participants and chunks of the foundation for the learning organization and its increasingly competitive capabilities.

Michael Beyerlein
Kristi Willbanks
Center for the Study of Work Teams at the
University of North Texas

REFERENCES

Brown, J. S., Collins, A., & Duguid, P. (1989). Situated cognition and the culture of learning. *Educational Researcher, 19,* pp. 32–42. http://www.ilt.columbia.edu/ilt/papers/JohnBrown.html

Kirkpatrick, D. L. (1972). *Evaluating training programs: The four levels.* San Francisco: Berrett-Koehler.

Knowles, M. S. (1992). *The adult learner: A neglected species* (4th ed). Houston, TX: Gulf.

O'Neil, M. (1996, August). *Do's and don'ts for the new trainer.* Info-Line 9608. Alexandria, VA: American Society for Training and Development.

Pinchot, G., & Pinchot, E. (1996). *The end of bureaucracy & the rise of the intelligent organization.* San Francisco: Berrett-Koehler.

Purser, R., & Montuori, A. (1995). Deconstructing the lone genius myth: Toward a contextual view of creativity. *Journal of Humanistic Psychology, 35*(3), 69–112.

Michael Beyerlein & Kristi Willbanks
Center for the Study of Work Teams
University of North Texas, Denton, Texas

PREFACE

"What you learn from experience you seldom forget."

This book provides you with fifty easy-to-use experiential activities for use in facilitating group dynamics and building relationships within teams. They are designed to allow participants to experience various interpersonal dynamics in a hands-on learning environment. By using these initiatives, individually or collectively, you can develop a complete one-day or two-day workshop to address a particular team's needs. These initiatives will provide you with a tool that puts team problem solving into action. Experience and self-discovery are the true teachers, and the participants are tasked to develop communication patterns and interactive styles required for effective problem solving.

These initiatives were developed for use either indoors or outdoors, requiring a variety of simple set-ups, with only a minimum of materials. The book provides a structure for the facilitator and his or her client to follow—from the time a request for training or an intervention is made through follow-up on what was learned. Suggested debriefing questions are provided, along with guiding principles for effective facilitation.

The facilitator's role in the process is to ask questions that stimulate the participants' understanding of the dynamics that occur. This interaction is referred to in this book as a "debriefing" session. A debriefing session is held after each activity, during which the facilitator asks group members specific questions relating to actions and behaviors that occurred and invites participants to share their reactions and apply what they have learned to other situations in life and at work.

This book was written by a facilitator, and each activity in this book has been used successfully numerous times in team-building workshops. The book is destined to become a valuable tool in your training tool box.

Ed Rose
Palm Bay, Florida
November 1998

ACKNOWLEDGMENTS

To assure a quality product for the user, I had my staff of professional facilitators review each activity as if they were going to use it with a team. This worked well with my first book, *Presenting and Training with Magic,* and I wanted to assure the same level of quality in this publication. To the following individuals who reviewed the referenced chapters and activities, I would like to say "Thank you":

Section One: Adaptable: Rick Manion

Section Two: Trustworthy: Mary Byrd

Section Three: Resourceful: John Burchinal

Section Four: Optimistic: Mark Sorensen

Section Five: Considerate: Mark Sorensen

Section Six: Warm-Ups & Miscellaneous: Ted LaRoche

I have been working with experiential learning initiatives since 1989, conducting team-building sessions and attending team-building workshops while visiting various experiential learning courses around the country. During my travels I have come into contact with some of the brightest minds in the field of experiential learning, directly or indirectly benefiting from my association with these talented individuals. Some of the activities in this book are adaptations of those I have experienced, and by no means am I trying to take credit for creating them. I have also included several traditional initiatives, updated for the 21st century.

Following is a list of some very special people in the world of experiential learning that I have learned from, and this is my acknowledgment of their direct or indirect contributions to this book:

Ray Green, president of Paradigm Communications, Tampa, Florida. On many occasions Ray has provided me critical help with various team-building events. He is the creator of Zodiak: The Game of Business Finance, which was a pioneer in experiential learning for financial training.

Sivasailam "Thiagi" Thiagarajan, Workshops by Thiagi, Bloomington, Indiana. I knew Thiagi only from his writings until I met him at the 1997 ASTD conference. We instantly felt a kinship, which became even stronger when we collaborated on a magic workshop and found our thoughts to be very synergistic. Thiagi is one of a kind. He has authored thirty-one books on improving human performance, mostly dealing with interactive experiential strategies. He is an energetic, warm, and friendly person who is an excellent professional in the field of management development and organizational design.

Brian Jackson, founder and director of The Orion Trust, Longwood, Florida. In my mind, Brian is the benchmark for a facilitator. He has industrial and commercial experience along with over twenty years' experience designing and developing experience-based programs for leadership development, much of that being international work designing and facilitating experience-based organizational performance programs for corporate clients. He has a highly interactive facilitation style, which he uses effectively with experience-based activities.

Tim Rumley, president of Dynamic Learning, Maitland, Florida. Tim is the author of *Not Just Games: Strategic Uses of Experiential Learning to Drive Business Results.*

Jeff Boyd, president of Operation Explore, in North Palm Beach, Florida. Jeff is an interesting and enthusiastic facilitator with whom I have had the pleasure of working or participating with in several team-building sessions.

Warren Cohen, management consultant, from Pinckney, Michigan. Warren and I have had several discussions on activities. He is a very creative individual who has some great ideas in the field of experiential learning.

Dr. Scott Simmerman, managing partner of Performance Management Company, Taylors, South Carolina. Scott is author of the Square Wheels tool kits and *The Search for the Lost Dutchman's Gold Mine.* He is a top-ranked international presenter on issues of leadership, team building, change, and management development.

Roger Woodgate is co-founder of ABA Consultants, Royston Herts, United Kingdom. The company provides both consulting and training services to clients in both Europe and the United States. Roger is a graduate of the University of London and was recently a Harkness Fellow of the Commonwealth Fund of New York. During his one-year fellowship in the United States, Roger examined "best practices" in the area of high-performance teams. He is author of a number of publications, the latest being a case study for ASTD's Developing High Performance Work Teams series.

Lim Peng Soon is the principal consultant of Learning and Performance Systems, based in Singapore. He works in partnership with organizations in designing and facilitating team-building and leadership programs using experiential learning methods to reach business objectives. He has spoken at various regional and international conferences, including the 1998 ASTD International Conference & Exposition in San Francisco. He has a passion for seeing growth and development in people. Peng is a self-proclaimed die-hard optimist and a lifelong learner.

Mike Winlaw is a founding partner of Network Australia, Brisbane, Queensland, an Australian-based organizational consulting group. Mike has specific expertise in managing team-based work forces and has assisted a number of clients along the team journey.

From personal experience, I have found these people to be experts in the field of experiential learning. They have all been a big help to me, either directly or indirectly. If you have a training need, they would be a great place to start.

ABOUT THE AUTHORS

Ed Rose is currently training manager at Harris Semiconductor in Palm Bay, Florida. He is a graduate of Warner Southern College with honors in organizational management. He is the author of *Presenting and Training with Magic* (McGraw-Hill, 1998) and numerous team-building activities. He has thirty-two years' experience in manufacturing, has served as quality examiner for the State of Florida, and has published numerous papers on the subject of self-directed work teams. He is a corporate practice expert with self-directed work teams for Harris Corporation and also a frequent presenter at American Society for Training and Development and Association for Quality and Participation national conferences, the University of North Texas International Conference on Work Teams, and others. He conducts workshops on team building for Harris throughout the United States and Europe.

Steve Buckley is currently senior training specialist at Harris Semiconductor in Palm Bay, Florida. He is a graduate of Indiana Vocational Technical College with a degree in computer programming. He is the editor and publisher of the Quality and Productivity Department newsletter at Harris. He edits and designs all manufacturing training materials produced at Harris Semiconductor, Palm Bay. He also assisted in the development of Ed Rose's book, *Presenting and Training with Magic*.

"We trained hard, but it seemed that every time we were beginning to form up into teams, we would be reorganized. I was to learn later in life that we tend to meet any new situation by reorganizing, and a wonderful method it can be for creating the illusion of progress while producing confusion, inefficiency and demoralization."

Gaius Petronius Arbiter
1ST CENTURY A.D.

Part 1

HOW TO USE THE INITIATIVES

Chapter 1 Introduction to Experiential Learning

In the past, success depended on what you, as an individual, could accomplish. It was simple: You completed tasks and either failed or succeeded. In today's world, success is measured by how you accomplish a task and whether you can do so within a team environment. Knowing how to work with others is crucial in order for a person to succeed. Businesses and other areas of society evaluate and reward people as a result of their team behaviors.

Are these behaviors taught in school? Are employees entering the workforce prepared for collaboration? Not usually. So how can someone learn to work in a team environment? By focusing on ways to build relationships among team members. Teamwork requires establishing common goals, sharing rewards, and agreeing on measures for success. The difference between success and failure sometimes is because of the "little things," like not having a good working relationship with other team members.

Unfortunately, many people believe that success is possible solely through the application of academically acquired intelligence. In Daniel Goleman's best-selling book, *Emotional Intelligence* (1998), he declares, "It's not your I.Q. that will be directly related to your success, it's your emotional intelligence quotient." Emotional intelligence (EQ) is defined as the ability to sense, understand, and apply the power and acumen of emotions as a source of human energy, information, trust, creativity, and influences.

The collective EQ of your team is far more important to its success than is its collective IQ. Emotional intelligence fuels the best decisions of the most dynamic and successful teams. It can make a major difference in the individual success of each team member and, subsequently, the overall success of the team. Measurable improvements in such critical areas as decision making, leadership, open communication, trusting relationships, and teamwork can be obtained by improving EQ-related competencies, such as self-awareness, self-control, empathy, effective listening, conflict management, collaboration, and cooperation.

Fortunately, EQ is learnable. It can be developed and improved at any time and at any age. Experiential learning can play a part in developing EQ, as it provides an environment that allows the participants to experience the behaviors relating to EQ listed above. The foundation of EQ is self-awareness. The experiential learning process allows participants to identify specific behaviors and actions that can be improved and learned by doing.

5

Stephen Covey's best-selling book, *The Seven Habits of Highly Effective People* (1989), addresses behaviors that support Goleman's emotional intelligence theory. It is important to understand Covey's concepts in order to develop "high performance work teams"—teams that consistently display the highest level of effective, productive behaviors and establish a trusting environment. Teams can progress into high-performance work teams regardless of their type or size. Personal experience has taught me that such levels of performance cannot be obtained without open and honest communication among team members. Developing effective personal interaction habits along with EQ provides the elements—paradigm flexibility, positive attitude, commitment, empathy, the ability to work with others, and a positive vision of the future—required for success.

We have used the following acronym successfully with teams over the last ten years: ATROC (Adaptable, Trustworthy, Resourceful, Optimistic, and Considerate). These five behaviors provide a good foundation for developing EQ. One very effective technique is to allow team members to experience various team dynamics through the use of experiential learning initiatives, allowing them to use their interaction skills, and to evaluate their experiences after each activity.

The intent of this book is to provide experiential activities that anyone can use in order to help develop desired team behaviors and improve EQ, in the process producing high-performance teams. The experiential learning activities should provide an effective tool to help you build relationships among a team or group of people.

I have used these initiatives many times over the past ten years at Harris Semiconductor, Palm Bay, Florida. Harris modified its traditional manufacturing environment, known for its "Theory X" management style (simply put, the farthest point on a continuum where "X" is directive and "Y" is participative) (McGregor, 1985), and transformed it into a model for team-based management. Many changes were introduced during this period that contributed to this successful transformation. Management leadership was critical to this success, but changing the way managers approached their responsibilities was another issue. They were asked to develop their leadership skills by doing less managing and more leading. These changes can be seen in the same context as improving emotional intelligence. Managers had to do the following:

- Become more aware of themselves (self-awareness),

- Develop a more empathetic approach to leading employees (self-control and empathy),

- Start listening to their employees more (effective listening), and

- Become collaborators in the team environment (conflict management and collaboration).

All of these were related to the elements Goleman identified. The initiatives and processes detailed in this book played a critical role in allowing Harris management personnel and employees to learn by doing.

The motto of experiential learning, "What you learn from experience you seldom forget," pinpoints the importance of learning from experience. Experiential learning generally begins in a training environment with a group of participants, preferably an established team or natural work group. The facilitator assigns the group a problem-solving task (an initiative), provides information to the team about the task to be completed, resource constraints, and the time limit. Following the instructional period, the team begins the initiative. During this phase of experiential learning, the facilitator observes the group dynamics that occur, as well as the process the team uses to complete the activity, then leads the group through a debriefing period, helping them to reflect on what transpired. This period of reflection allows self-discovery learning to occur.

The initiatives in this book were developed around the ATROC model listed above and are organized accordingly. It has been pointed out to me that many of these activities can be used interchangeably. Although that is absolutely correct, I have tried to structure the debriefing questions to bring out the particular ATROC behavior the initiative is listed under.

So, what does ATROC mean? The basic theory is not rocket science, and I have not uncovered any great secret. In some cases you may not see the direct connection between an initiative and the behavior I placed it under; please don't spend a lot of time debating this in your mind. This is simply my way of organizing my thoughts, and I believe it will help facilitate the use of the book. The types of initiatives and the effective behaviors they are intended to help participants learn are described below.

Adaptable. Initiatives that highlight communication, planning, and various group dynamics are associated with positive change. Team members must be adaptable in order to change. Charles Darwin said, "It's not the strongest of the species, nor the most intelligent, that survive; it's the ones most responsive to change." An adaptable team member must have a positive attitude toward team goals and activities. He or she should be flexible in planning and problem solving.

Too many times teams take action before they take time to plan. If they fail to plan, they are in effect planning to fail. High-performance teams take time to plan before taking action. Open and honest communication with others on the team is encouraged. And let's not forget attitude. As long ago as A.D. 60, Epictetus said, "It's not what happens to us that affects us, it's our attitude toward it that does." Attitude can be considered the control panel of our lives.

Trustworthy. These initiatives highlight trust and mutual respect. Trust is the foundation of all human relationships. Teamwork is about those human relationships among team members, and so each team member earns trust by doing what he or she commits to. An environment must be created in which members feel safe—even to fail. To create such an environment, emphasize the strengths of the team and support the weaknesses by coaching and encouraging.

Encouragement is oxygen for the soul. Let others know you appreciate them. Recognize each team member's contributions. Establish an environment in which each team member is accountable for his or her actions, maintains and enhances others' self-esteem, and has the discipline to perform at his or her best.

Resourceful. Initiatives that highlight creativity, innovation, and breakthrough thinking. To survive, we all must be resourceful. In today's world of high technology and speed, we are inundated with data. This is indeed the "information age"; successful people and organizations must rely on the collective intelligence of teams. It is time to break down perceived barriers within organizations and relationships and to ask for help from others. Become a lifetime learner, and always be open to new ideas.

Optimistic. Optimistic initiatives move beyond perceived limits, challenging biases, managing conflicts, and increasing self-awareness. More than three hundred years ago, Spinoza said, "As long as we believe something is impossible it will be; the moment we see it as possible, we change our lives." It is equally true today. Optimism is similar to attitude, but deals more with the power to envision and plan for a positive future by not letting perceived limitations interfere. Yogi Berra said, "You can't steal second base with your foot on first." Challenge yourself and your biases. Once we understand ourselves, we have a better chance of understanding our interactions with others and of managing conflicts more effectively.

Considerate. Initiatives that highlight creativity, teamwork, cooperation, and collaboration. Those initiatives teach participants to be considerate of others. Consideration is the glue that allows relationships to work. It is important to value all team members' inputs. Sometimes what looks like a bizarre suggestion can turn out to be a great approach to the solution of a problem.

Creativity is only possible in an environment in which team members can be free to express themselves. Cooperation and collaboration behaviors show consideration of others, and this generates mutual respect, the foundation of trust. For effective problem solving, the team must consider all options and, in some cases, be willing to take one step backward in order to go forward.

The ATROC acronym reminds us to focus on specific aspects of team dynamics. As you become more comfortable with the process and the initiatives, you will discover their depth and many additional uses. Success (or failure) of these types of initiatives is closely tied to the techniques and style of the facilitator, who can make the participants feel that their time was well spent or completely wasted. It is a big responsibility. However, I'm sure you are up to the task, and this book provides the initiatives that have helped improve the EQ levels of the employees at Harris Semiconductor, who have made the successful transition to team-based management. The initiatives contained in this book have been proven to allow team members to learn by doing.

Chapter Two provides techniques and general guidelines for conducting a successful session.

REFERENCES

Covey, S. (1989). *The seven habits of highly effective people.* New York: Simon & Schuster.

Goleman, D. (1998). *Emotional intelligence.* New York: Bantam.

McGregor, D., & Bennis, W. (1985). *Human side of enterprise: 25th anniversary edition.* New York: McGraw-Hill.

CHAPTER 2

TECHNIQUES FOR FACILITATING EXPERIENTIAL LEARNING

"What we sow or plant in soil will come back to us in exact kind. It's impossible to sow corn and get a crop of wheat, but we entirely disregard this law when it comes to mental sowing."

Stephen Covey

THE HARVEST

The success of experiential learning initiatives, whether simple or complex, is a direct result of the effectiveness of facilitator interaction before, during, and after the session. Consequently, facilitators must "sow" what they want to "harvest." Companies can easily spend thousands of dollars on outside consultants for team-building workshops and team development materials, but overall success will be based on the ability of the group's facilitator to work well with the group. A good experiential learning facilitator is worth every cent he or she is paid. Good facilitators relate well with participants and incorporate and utilize initiatives to ensure that participants leave with something that they did not previously have. Facilitation is not difficult if one uses the right tools, coupled with the correct interactive disciplines.

Helpful techniques and debriefing questions are supplied in this chapter for use during and after experiential learning initiatives. Your comfort level with these will increase with experience. Remember that the facilitator's role is to lead the discussion, not to tell the participants how they should feel or react. Let's try a brief exercise to make the point.

Write down the answers to the following questions:

1. Think of a number between 1 and 10.

   _____

2. Multiply that number by 2.

   _____

3. Add 8 to your answer.

_____

4. Divide that number by 2.

_____

5. Subtract your original number from your answer.

_____

6. Convert your number to a letter: 1 = A; 2 = B; 3 = C; 4 = D; 5 = E; and so on.
7. Think of a European country whose name begins with the letter you now have.
8. Think of an animal that starts with the last letter in that country's name.
9. Think of a fruit that starts with the last letter of that animal's name.

Is it possible that you were thinking "orange kangaroos in Denmark"? How could I know what you were thinking?

What does this exercise show? It is an example of the role of the facilitator. Your role as facilitator does not permit you to direct participants about how to solve initiatives or tell them what they have learned. A facilitator is a modern-day Socrates, simply asking the questions during the debriefing session that guide discovery learning for the participants. As a farmer's preparation, approach, and execution of crop planting make for a successful harvest, the facilitator plants a learning crop. The amount of knowledge participants gain from experiential learning initiatives is in direct proportion to how a facilitator prepares those initiatives and incorporates specific debriefing questions to help them uncover the learning objectives ("front-loading" the initiative). A debriefing session for a facilitator is as a harvest for a farmer. A facilitator must provide structure and observe behaviors in order to become a successful "farmer" of self-discovery learning, which transfers to the workplace.

THE FACILITATION PROCESS

The following is the typical process a facilitator must follow when using experiential initiatives:

1. The facilitator presents the initiative to the participants, either verbally or in writing. By presenting the task in writing, the facilitator offers additional communication difficulties and creates some interesting points to introduce during a debriefing session. Handouts are provided in this book for that purpose.

2. The team undertakes the initiative, focusing on the process rather than on success or failure.

3. After participants complete the initiative, the facilitator leads a debriefing session, which is the key to the process. The harvesting of learning begins during this time. The discussion focuses on what occurred during the activity, what participants learned, and how they can apply the lessons learned to real-life situations.

The following basic rules for effective facilitation provide a solid foundation:

- Safety first! Never assume anything.
- Be yourself and display positive body language.
- Believe in what you are doing and in the value of experiential learning.
- Serve as a role model of attentiveness, empathy, energy, and participation.
- Offer and display unconditional respect for others, as well as for yourself. Expect the same from others.
- Encourage cooperation and discourage competition.
- Allow participants to choose whether they want to participate.

These rules provide a way to build an environment for each initiative with open and honest communication on all levels. Such communication promotes a successful debriefing.

The facilitator also must use the following guidelines during the initiative and debriefing session to ensure a harvest of self-discovery learning for each participant:

1. Front-load the initiative, that is, plant the seeds and fertilize the crop (the learning objectives) by:
   - Pre-planning the initiative after identifying the client's objectives.
   - Selecting an initiative that addresses the appropriate learning points and guiding it in the proper direction.
   - Ensuring that participants understand the objectives. (In some cases, however, you may choose to be vague because you want the participants to work through a process without any preconceptions.)
   - Taking detailed notes during the initiative to ensure a productive debriefing.
   - Highlighting the learning objectives that have been identified by asking the appropriate questions during the debriefing.
2. Establish a clear contract with the group concerning the activity. (See the Experiential Contract (Form C2.1) and Debriefing Contract (Form C2.2) in the Appendix, beginning on page 249.)
3. Allow participants to interact with one another in a nonacademic, nonwork, and nonthreatening environment.
4. Allow team members to discover the importance of individual contributions within a team environment.
5. Conduct activities in a way that allows participants to have fun while learning.
6. Give praise sparingly and as appropriate, using the following guidelines:
   - Make sure that participants understand why they are receiving praise when you choose to provide it.
   - Balance the amount of praise you give because some participants could perceive praise of others (or lack of praise for themselves) as negative judgments about their own performance.

- Be careful not to overdo it, as participants may begin to doubt your sincerity.

7. Encourage each individual to participate, even if it is only in a coaching role.

8. Protect participants' self-esteem throughout the process by avoiding a win/lose focus.

9. Maintain a high energy level, stay alert, and stay focused on the intended harvest (the learning objectives), as facilitator style and attitude greatly influence how participants will receive the initiative.

THE DEBRIEFING

It is important for all participants to discuss their feelings after an initiative. Initiatives may last only fifteen minutes, but a good debriefing session on that fifteen-minute initiative could last for an hour or more. The length of the session depends on the facilitator and his or her perception of the energy level of the group. Each initiative in this book offers recommended debriefing times as a reference only. Always consider group involvement and energy levels. A debriefing session is coming to an end when the group's energy level decreases.

A facilitator's focus during a debriefing should be on ensuring clarification and reflection to maximize learning. Meaningful learning occurs when the participants can relate an initiative to their real-life work environment.

Use the following ten rules as a guide for conducting an effective debriefing:

1. Have the group sit in a circle.

2. Encourage people to communicate their feelings openly. Be sensitive to strong personalities that might dominate the session and to possible group dynamics that could prevent some people from participating.

3. Use body language (eye contact, head movements, and so on) and verbal responses ("yes," "tell us more," and similar responses) to validate the comments of group members. Direct your attention to the person speaking, asking that only one person speak at a time. Make sure that everyone can hear (and be heard) and that everyone has an opportunity to share inputs and observations.

4. Facilitate discussion by encouraging people's responses on particular points that highlight the learning objectives for the initiative.

5. When necessary, confront situations in which behaviors are counterproductive to group processing. Avoid singling out a person, but do focus on any person's unacceptable behavior.

6. Have the group reflect on the experience by relating any learning or self-discoveries back to their jobs.

7. Do not permit any degrading or insulting comments.

8. Do not force participation—encourage, but don't force! Set and expand ground rules for participating as required.

9. Avoid the word "should" during debriefing sessions.

10. Take care not to belittle or "talk down" to participants. Remain neutral and see and experience what they do. Do not force the participants to see things the way you do; allow them to think for themselves and discover their own learning points. Your role is to shape the impressions of the participants in order to provide maximum opportunities for self-discovery.

General Questions for a Debriefing

Although specific questions are provided with each initiative, you can also select questions from the following list if desired. Use these questions as a way to get things started and keep the group focused. As participants begin expressing their feelings, allow the group to evolve naturally to its own level, keeping the discussion focused on the objectives established for the initiatives. Ask yourself, "What is it I want to harvest in terms of learning?"

Depending on your response, any of the following questions could be used:

- Rate your teamwork on a scale from 1 to 10. What factors contributed to your rating?
- What communications system(s) did the team establish? How successful were they?
- Did team members support one another? In what ways?
- What do you feel your team has learned from this activity?
- Were there benefits to working as a team? What were they?
- Were there any drawbacks to working as a team? What were they?
- How was leadership handled?
- Did participants exhibit leadership behaviors? What were they?
- Was leadership shared in any way? How was this accomplished?
- What did each person contribute to the solution to the problem?
- Can you think of a time when someone in the group expressed a strong feeling non-verbally? How?
- Do you feel that others in the group listened to what you said? What made you believe this?
- Did all member(s) become part of the group? How did the group try to encourage members to participate?
- What team members' behaviors did you observe that made the team more effective? Less effective?
- Were suggestions made and not heard or acted on by the group? What were they?
- Was there any pressure to perform? How did it manifest itself?
- What was your goal? Did every team member know the goal? Did everyone have the same understanding of the goal?
- What strengths did you personally contribute to the group?
- Whose contributions did you appreciate?

- Whose contributions bothered you? In what way?
- What would you change if you could do it over? Why or why not?
- How does this activity relate back to the real world?
- What did you personally learn from this activity? How did you feel when it was finished?
- What did you learn or relearn about yourself from this activity?
- How would you change this initiative if you were the facilitator?

Four Phases of Experiential Debriefing*: Feeling, Transpiration, Agreement, and Transference

Four phases of self-discovery learning must be considered when choosing questions to reinforce pre-selected objectives.

Feeling. The first phase focuses on the participants' personal feelings about the outcome of an initiative. The following question can be used as a focal point: "How do you feel about the outcome of this initiative?"

Transpiration. The second phase requires participants to present an accurate account of what transpired during an initiative. Facilitators take notes during the initiative to use throughout this phase, in order to record team dynamics or to identify a particular person's statement or behavior. When the facilitator provides specifics, participants feel some responsibility to respond and they become comfortable. A facilitator who utilizes specifics establishes a personal connection with the group, thus increasing the effectiveness of the session.

Agreement. The third phase requires the group to further develop their feelings. Participants agree or disagree about the meaning and particular aspects of events that have transpired. The goal is participant agreement, but it is acceptable to "agree to disagree," as some participants may not ever agree.

Transference. The fourth phase is the most significant for facilitator success and participant self-discovery. Transference begins with the participants identifying what they can learn from the experience and how they can adapt that same learning to their work environments. A good question to ask at this point might be, "Now that we've reached an agreement on what occurred, how can that information be transferred into the workplace?"

Now let's move on to Chapter Three, where you will learn how to use the initiatives in this book.

---

*The four phases of experiential debriefing listed here are modeled from the original philosophical concepts of Sivasailam Thiagarajan.

CHAPTER 3 HOW TO USE INITIATIVES

Would a doctor prescribe medication before knowing what was wrong with a patient? Not likely. First the doctor would review a patient's symptoms, order tests, and analyze findings before offering a diagnosis and prescribing medication. In this way a doctor and a facilitator have some things in common. Both must know what is wrong with a "patient" in order to prescribe the correct "medicine." A facilitator might prescribe an initiative that will help participants understand the group dynamics causing problems within a team—dynamics that may be either visible or invisible to the team members.

The facilitator must gather data so that he or she can provide assistance during the initiative and ask relevant questions during the debriefing session. Chapter Two provided you with rules, guidelines, and general questions for facilitating an initiative; this chapter provides a seven-step structured approach for planning an experiential learning experience.

Step 1: Meet with the Client

The first thing to do is to arrange a time to meet with the client to discuss and complete the Team-Building Intervention Worksheet (Form C3.1 in the Appendix). The completed form will provide information so that you can structure, direct, and facilitate the day's activities. The form is divided into several sections:

- *Section A: Team Needs.* Review the behavioral issue(s) for which the client is seeking help. Find out the needs of the group, and the behaviors and issues that are preventing the team from being productive. Once you and your client reach an agreement regarding the issues that need to be addressed, identify time constraints. How much time should be allotted for this activity? A day? Four hours? Two hours? Also decide where the training session will be conducted.

- *Section B: Team Objectives.* You and the client must now decide what objectives are to be addressed. Set clear expectations for the desired outcomes. Agreement between you and your client is crucial for success.

- *Section C: Recommended Facilitator Interventions.* Complete this section after reviewing the fifty initiatives listed in the table of contents to this book. For example, if the group has issues with communication, team trust, and cooperation, then choose initiatives that address those issues. Let's say that the client wants to use a full workday for the session. Find initiatives that both address the issues and fit the time constraints and list them under Section C.

- *Section D: Initiatives/Objectives/Metaphors.* After you have listed the initiatives you selected in Section C, decide which will best address the objectives you want to accomplish. You and your client may also develop metaphors, symbols, or stories to support these initiatives. First list the initiatives and objectives, then the metaphors and symbols that may help you bring your learning points alive and help the participants embrace them. Be sure to incorporate personal examples and metaphors that employees can relate to. This section will be helpful for reference during the debriefing session.

- *Section E: Safety Considerations.* Safety should be a primary concern, so list safety considerations based on the tasks, participants, and training site. The initiatives in this book should not provide major physical problems or prove to be hazardous for anyone. However, always consider your participants and their abilities to perform the tasks required by the initiative. Remember to "challenge by choice," allowing the participants the option to take part or not, or to participate as a coach or observer.

- *Section F: Team Members' Issues.* List the team members by name and include any physical restrictions they may have. The Americans with Disabilities Act requires that all employees be given the opportunity to participate in company activities, so information about physical restrictions should be used to help you develop a successful workshop.

- *Section G: Materials Required.* Review each activity you have chosen and list all the materials required. Have all materials ready prior to every initiative.

Use your completed copy of Form C3.1 to organize and prepare for the day's events.

Step 2: Plan the Session

Based on your discussion with the client and the completed Team-Building Intervention Worksheet (Form C3.1), plan how you will conduct the session, including room set-up, breaks, and timing of all steps.

Step 3: Prepare Materials

Gather and prepare all materials you will need and plan the logistics for the initiatives carefully. You are then ready to conduct the session.

Step 4: Conduct the Session

Step-by-step instructions for conducting each initiative are provided, so you can now conduct the session.

Step 5: Evaluate the Session

After the session is over, hand out the Learning Experience Evaluation (Form C3.2 in the Appendix) to all participants. Be sure to have participants complete the form immediately while their feelings about the experience and what they have learned are fresh in their minds.

Step 6: Complete Debriefing

Complete the Facilitator's Debriefing Notes (Form C3.3 in the Appendix), using participants' feedback and your own experience and observations of the session. Review the Learning Experience Evaluations (Form C3.2) that you have collected from participants and your Facilitator's Debriefing Notes (C3.3) for ways to improve or modify the initiatives and your facilitation in the future. Keep all paperwork for future reference, especially since the client may ask to use your services again. This way you will not accidentally use the same initiatives a second time with a group.

Step 7: Distribute Follow-Up Survey

Distribute the Follow-Up Survey (Form C3.4 in the Appendix) to all participants approximately four weeks after the initiative and debriefing have taken place. This process not only helps you, but also the participants and clients as well. Record the feedback so that you can modify the initiative at a later date if desired in order to make it more effective. As with any survey, persuading participants to return their completed forms could be a problem. Be mindful of this and suggest that the client offer incentives to its employees for completing their surveys or, if e-mail is available, it could be used to help raise the response rate.

Using the forms in the Appendix allows you to keep track of initiatives used, the teams you have used them with, and the results of your training sessions. It provides a way to learn to identify similar symptoms, patterns, and behaviors that may help you assist future clients and guard against repeating the same initiative with the same team.

I have found success with this process, and I hope you find the same value in it. Again, remember that you will harvest what you plant. A good harvest only occurs if you take the proper steps to assure success. Good farmers learn from years of experience and know what to do to obtain a good crop. Using the structure in this chapter will allow you to utilize experiential learning initiatives as an effective team-building tool within your organization.

I have ended each activity with a quote. The right quote can add great insight. They are listed in this book to stimulate your thoughts as a facilitator. If you feel that you can effectively use them during debriefing, please do. I hope they work for you as well as they have for me.

Part 2

THE
INITIATIVES

#1 SILENT PLANNING

OVERVIEW

Participants must organize themselves into birth order according to month and day without talking.

OBJECTIVES

- To develop creative communication skills
- To help team members understand the concept of adaptability

GROUP SIZE

Eight to one hundred participants in groups of four to ten

MATERIALS

A method for timing the initiative

PHYSICAL SET-UP

A room with enough space to accommodate the number of small groups without distraction

SUGGESTED TIME

36 minutes (16-minute activity with a 20-minute debriefing)

PROCEDURE

1. Separate participants into groups of four to ten members each, depending on the size of the group. Use your best judgment for group size.
2. Explain to the groups that the goal of this activity is for members to line up in order by birth month and day. Tell participants that if two (or more) of them share the

same birthday that they should arrange themselves by height, from shortest to tallest. Finally, instruct the groups that they are to conduct this exercise *without talking*.

> *NOTE:* The main idea is for the groups to process the instructions and complete the initiative without requesting directions from you.

3. Advise everyone that successful teams complete this birth-order exercise in less than 15 minutes.

4. Tell the groups to begin.

5. Do not volunteer advice or assistance.

6. Observe each group and take specific notes for use during the debriefing session.

7. When they have finished, or the 15 minutes have ended, conduct a debriefing session using the following questions:

   - What type of problems did your team experience?
   - How can you relate this simple task to real work problems?
   - What made your team successful? Unsuccessful? Explain.
   - What did you learn from this activity?
   - In what ways did this activity parallel your current work environment? What insights can you take back to the job?

8. Tell everyone any observations you had, and allow the group to absorb the significance of your observations. Allow time for constructive criticism, agreement, and disagreement.

QUOTE

"Character is like a photograph; it develops in the dark."

Unknown

#2   A COMMON VISION

OVERVIEW

Participants must work together as a team and move from Point A to Point B while they are roped together with each facing in a different direction.

OBJECTIVES

- To experience the dynamics of working as a team
- To experience the viewpoints of others when completing a task
- To demonstrate that reaching a team goal is easier when all members have the same vision

GROUP SIZE

Eight to twenty-five participants

MATERIALS

- A 25-foot length of rope
- One blindfold for each participant (if you use the variation)
- A method for timing the initiative

PHYSICAL SET-UP

A large open area, about 25 yards wide

SUGGESTED TIME

80 minutes (40-minute activity with a 40-minute debriefing)

PROCEDURE

1. Prior to the activity, identify two locations, Point A and Point B, that are at least 10 feet apart. The distance will depend on the amount of space and time available. One is the starting point, A, the other the ending point, B. Mark them in some way.

2. Ask all the participants to gather together into a circular group at Point A, with each participant facing a different direction.

> NOTE: Stress that everyone must be facing in a different direction. Some participants will immediately see that this will make it difficult for them to move toward their goal. Others will not.

3. After everyone has formed the circular group, have them pass the rope around the outside of the circle and secure the ends of the rope so that the group is tied in a bundle.

4. Inform the participants that their goal is to move the entire group from Point A to Point B.

5. Instruct them to begin.

6. When they have finished (or the 40 minutes have expired), conduct a debriefing session using the following questions:

   - Did your team experience any difficulty when you had to move in one direction while facing in different directions?

   - What problems did you experience?

   - Did your team have a common purpose?

   - Did your team have the same vision (relating to your final destination)?

   - (If the variation was used) How did the additional constraint of not being able to see affect the team?

   - What did your team do that was effective? Ineffective?

   - In what ways does this activity parallel your current work environment? What insights can you take back to the job?

VARIATION

After you have given the instructions, but before the participants have begun the initiative, you may elect to blindfold (a) all of the participants or (b) all but three of the participants.

QUOTE

"Vision without action is merely a dream. Action without vision just passes the time. Vision with action can change the world."

Joel Barker

#3 NOAH'S ARK

OVERVIEW

The whole team must simultaneously move off the ground onto a set of concrete blocks and stay there for as long as possible without assistance from any inanimate objects. There is also a hidden resource that will make the task easier: an extra cement block. The team members must depend on one another and their ability to think "outside the box" and seek win-win solutions.

OBJECTIVES

- To encourage team members to demonstrate positive group behaviors (collaboration)
- To recognize the need for adaptability
- To learn that effective communication is essential to good planning
- To help team members use their creativity
- To demonstrate the importance of knowing all of a team's resources

GROUP SIZE

Twelve to sixteen participants in two equal-sized teams

MATERIALS

- Two cement blocks per team
- One additional cement block marked with a red "S" (for "spare")
- One Handout 3.1: Noah's Ark Instructions for Teams for each team
- A method for timing the initiative

PHYSICAL SET-UP

Outdoors. Separate the teams so that they can see each other but must go out of their way to communicate with one another.

SUGGESTED TIME

30 minutes (10-minute activity with a 20-minute debriefing)

PROCEDURE

1. Before bringing the group to the area, set the two cement blocks for each team right next to one another on soft, level ground in an area away from trees or other objects that the team might use to support themselves, and put the "S" block somewhere between the areas where the two teams will be located. This spare block should be hidden slightly, but easy enough to find if participants look for it. Make sure that there will be enough space between the two teams so that they will not interfere with one another.

2. When you are ready to begin, bring the group to the prepared area and separate the participants into two teams. Give each team a copy of Handout 3.1 to read, and ask them to begin reading it.

> NOTE: If anyone has a problem participating in the exercise, have him or her coach or observe. As facilitator, be ready to do some spotting yourself.

3. Take notes as the teams proceed regarding group dynamics and behavior.

4. Do not volunteer any assistance. Answer questions only if team members ask for clarification.

> NOTE: The key learning point is that a team should always gather its resources and have a full understanding of the extent and the scope of a problem before addressing it. Sometimes a team has to realize that the simplest way to solve a problem is to look around for extra resources and to build constructive working alliances with fellow teams.

5. Instruct the participants to begin.

6. After the allotted 10 minutes are up, conduct a debriefing session using the following questions:

- Did you feel any sense of competition?
- What was your mission?
- How creatively did your team use the available blocks?
- Did the two teams collaborate and look for a win-win solution?
  - Did collaboration help?
  - If not, why not?
  - What were the problems?
  - Did anyone suggest collaboration? What happened?
  - Would it have been easier to solve the problem if the teams had collaborated?
  - Did you feel you were a member of one team or two separate teams? What contributed to this feeling?
- Did any team have a competitive advantage?
- If your team did not find the extra block, why do you think that was?
- If you were an observer, what did you observe?
- What are some parallels with the way you conduct your day-to-day work?
- What have you learned from this initiative that you will be able to apply to your current work environment?

> NOTE: If the participants do not locate the spare block, inform them that sometimes we fail to search out the resources available.

QUOTE

"There is nothing more dangerous than an idea when it's the only one you have."

Unknown

NOAH'S ARK INSTRUCTIONS FOR TEAMS

Your task is to get your entire team simultaneously off the ground and onto the cement block(s) and keep the team there for as long as possible.

Be mindful of the following constraints:

- You can only use the top surface of the block(s).
- No feet or other body parts may touch the sides of the block(s) or the ground.

You may use only the following resources:

- Team members
- The block(s)
- Up to 10 minutes

#4 SQUARES AND MORE SQUARES*

OVERVIEW

Participants working in small teams are asked to form as many squares of equal size as possible from a number of geometric shapes provided. The environment is competitive; participants are not allowed to observe how other teams are performing the task. The best solution involves not only good planning skills, but an ability to "think outside the box."

OBJECTIVE

- To demonstrate the need for benchmarking, critical thinking, and planning in the workplace

GROUP SIZE

Ten to twenty participants divided into five teams of at least two participants each

MATERIALS

- Geometric shapes cut from the pattern on the five templates (eight sets of the five templates for a total of 120 shapes)
- A flip chart or overhead transparency of Handout 4.1
- A flip chart or overhead transparency of Handout 4.2
- A copy of Handout 4.3 for the facilitator
- A method for timing the initiative

PHYSICAL SET-UP

Indoors, in an area with space enough to allow teams to spread out and work unobserved by other teams

---

*This initiative is from Mike Winlaw, Network Australia Organizational Consulting Group Pty Ltd.

SUGGESTED TIME

75 minutes (45-minute activity with 30-minute debriefing)

PROCEDURE

1. Prior to the initiative, prepare the shapes as follows. Make eight copies of each of the five templates. Cut the copies apart on the solid lines, making sure no lines show on the pieces. When you are finished, you will have a total of 120 shapes.

2. To begin the activity, place the shapes in a pile in the center of the room. It is preferable that only one of the small squares be clearly visible near the top of the pile. The pile should be about 18 inches across in size.

3. Separate the participants into teams of roughly equal size, preferably with many smaller teams rather than a few larger teams.

4. Post the instructions from Handout 4.1. Direct participants to read the instructions and make sure that everyone understands them.

5. Tell the participants that you will not answer any questions during the activity itself.

6. Instruct the teams to begin the planning portion of the activity and inform all teams when the 10 minutes are up.

7. Next tell the teams to choose one member to select each team's pieces and to proceed with the selection process as per the instructions. At this point teams may choose to put up barriers, such as chairs, around their work.

8. Remind the teams that there is to be *no talking* while assembling squares. Tell the teams that they have 3 minutes to conduct the activity, and instruct them to begin.

> *NOTE:* Do not let the teams see the work of other teams.

9. When the 3 minutes have expired, count the number of squares each team has formed. Count only the squares that are of equal size. (For example, a team may have three large squares and four small squares, so their result is four.)

10. Post Handout 4.2 and record each team's score for Round 1 on the sheet.

11. Tell the teams you will give them an opportunity to better their scores. Inform them that there will be another 3-minute round, but this time team members may communicate with one another, *but not with members of other teams.* By now, some teams will be picking up on the checkerboard pattern solution.

> *NOTE:* This round may be omitted if you are short of time.

12. Count and record the results for Round 2.

13. Now tell the teams that they will do some "benchmarking." They will be permitted to walk around the room and look at other teams' squares. Allow a few minutes for this activity.

14. Tell the teams that they will now have a third chance at the activity, and that this time team members can communicate among themselves and with other teams' members for 3 minutes.

15. After Round 3, count each team's squares and record the results.

16. (Optional) If you have time, take the activity a step further and allow the teams to rotate to another team's shapes to see whether they can be more effective with those shapes, that is, can they beat that team's score?

17. Conduct a debriefing session using the following questions:

    • How good were your planning skills? Did you have a fallback strategy if the shapes you wanted were not there when it was your turn to choose?

    • How successful were you as a team? How did your team define "success"?

    • How would you rate your team's level of critical thinking? How long did it take for your team to realize that you needed to think "outside the box" in order to find the best solution?

    • What was your reaction when your team's performance was reviewed? How did you feel when your team's score was posted? (Some teams may be frustrated when you count fewer squares than the number of squares they think they have formed. These will be the teams who did not focus on the words "equal size.")

    • Did the benchmarking help?

    • Were there issues about role clarity? Who took the lead?

    • What were the key learning points of this experience for you as an individual?

    • How can you relate this initiative back to your current work environment?

QUOTE

"Thinking is the hardest work there is, which is the probable reason so few engage in it."

Henry Ford

SQUARES AND MORE SQUARES TASK

Objective

- To form as many squares of equal size as you can, utilizing the pieces provided in competition with other teams.

Planning Period

10 minutes

- During the planning period one person at a time from your team may view the pieces provided, but cannot touch them.

- During this time, team members may discuss strategy for the selection process, but do not let other teams overhear your discussion.

- At the end of the planning period, your team will choose a representative for the selection process. Each team's representative will select five pieces at a time for a total of twenty pieces per team.

Building Time

3 minutes

The following constraints apply:

- You cannot cut, tear, bend, or overlay the pieces.

- You cannot trade your pieces with other teams.

- A square has four equal sides and must have four clearly defined boundaries.

- The display must be static.

- You cannot look at other teams' work at any stage during the activity, and you may hide your own work in some way.

- During the building time, your team cannot talk either to one another or to other teams' members.

SQUARES AND MORE SQUARES TALLY

Key: 0 – 5 squares = Poor

6 – 12 squares = Average

13 – 20 squares = Good

21+ squares = Excellent

TEAM	Round 1	Round 2	Round 3

SQUARES AND MORE SQUARES TEMPLATE 1

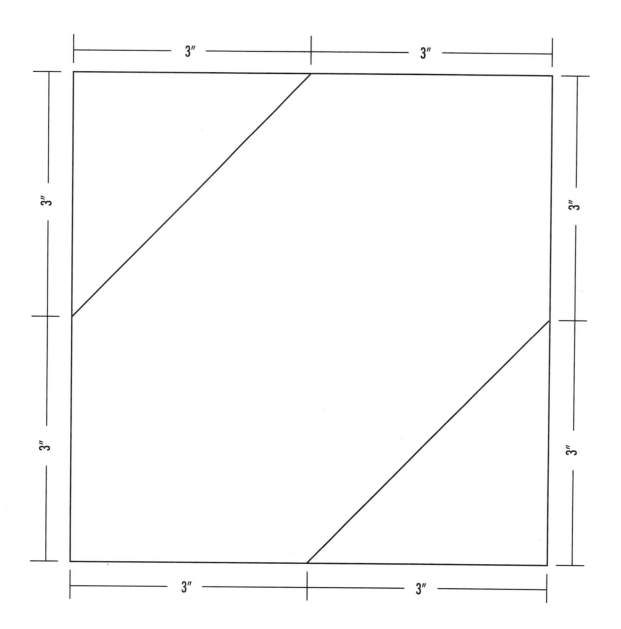

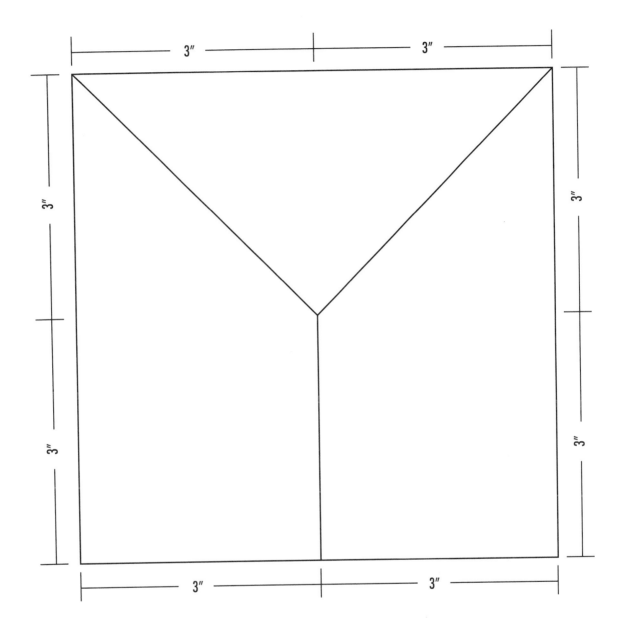

SQUARES AND MORE SQUARES TEMPLATE 3

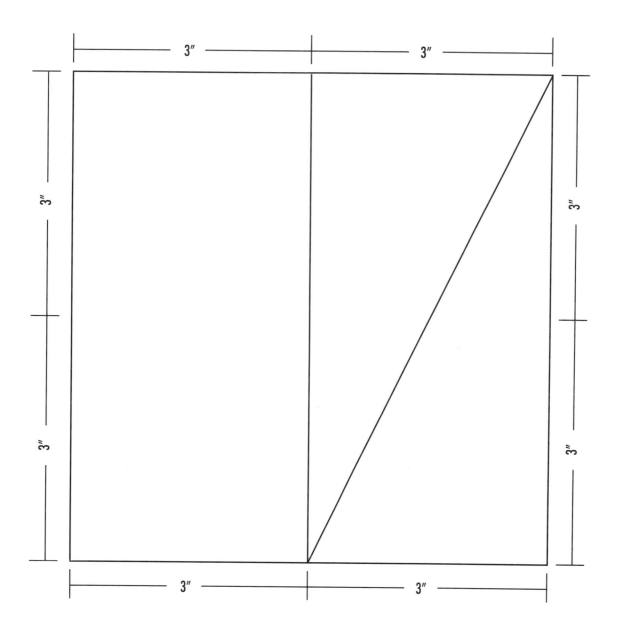

SQUARES AND MORE SQUARES TEMPLATE 4

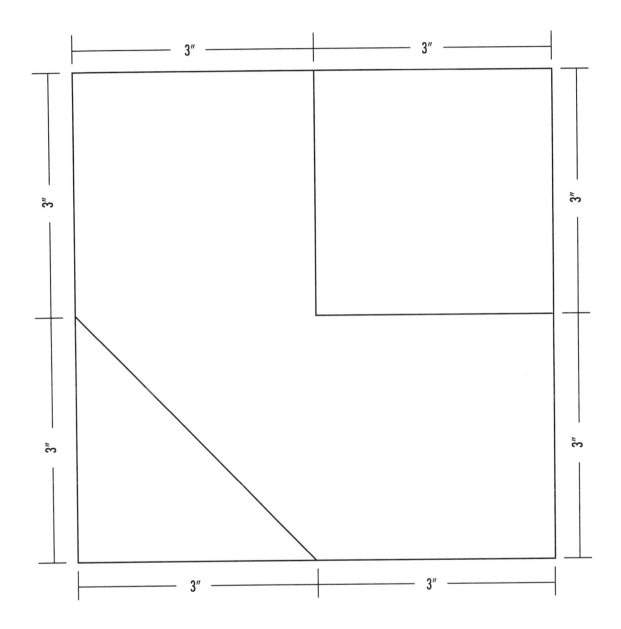

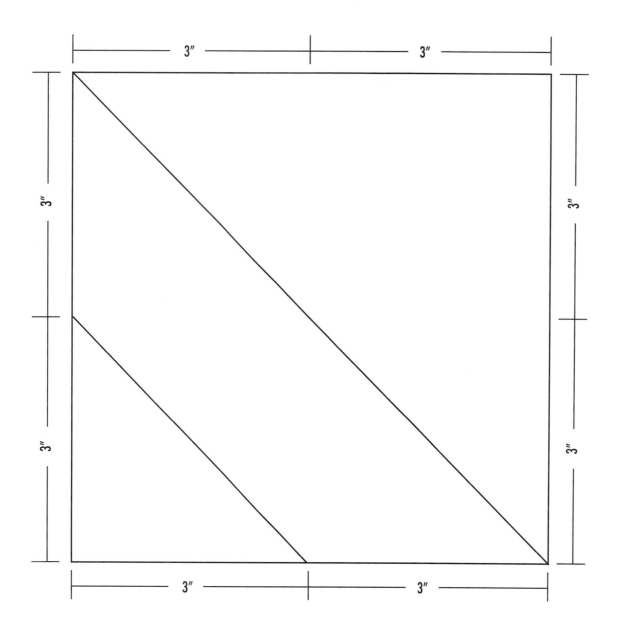

SQUARES AND MORE SQUARES SOLUTION

As a general rule, very few teams will realize that the objective of the game calls for squares of equal size; most teams will form a number of squares of varying sizes. The best result we have seen for this activity was twenty-six squares of equal size on the first pass.

A solution in which the pieces form a checkerboard pattern—with the empty spaces forming squares of equal sizes (which are also counted) between the pieces forming squares of equal sizes—is the most effective. See the example below showing nine completed squares.

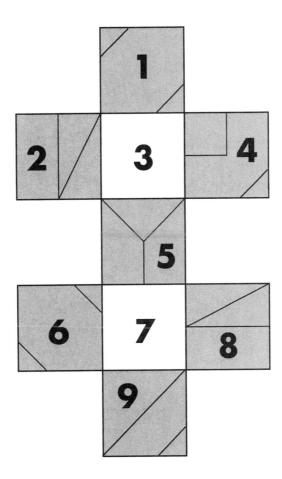

#5 CANYON OF NO RETURN*

OVERVIEW

This team initiative is focused on establishing effective communication methods and developing plans. The group's personal resources are limited, and they must work together in order to achieve their goal.

OBJECTIVES

- To experience the difficulty of developing a plan with certain physical constraints
- To experience a task that requires adapting to the environment
- To develop alternative communication systems
- To demonstrate the importance of effective communication within a group

GROUP SIZE

Eight to ten participants per team

MATERIALS

- Copies of Handout 5.1 for half of the participants
- Enough blindfolds so that half of the group can be blindfolded
- Two 1-inch × 10-inch × 8-foot boards for marking the "canyon" (If boards are not available, other materials such as rope may be used.)
- A 35-foot length of heavy rope
- One bucket
- A water supply for filling the bucket
- A method for timing the initiative

---

*This activity is adapted from an exercise by Brian Jackson of The Orion Trust.

PHYSICAL SET-UP

This initiative must be conducted outdoors and requires a sturdy tree.

SUGGESTED TIME

50 minutes (20-minute activity with a 30-minute debriefing)

PROCEDURE

> *NOTE:* Spotting (both by the facilitator and by participants) is *imperative,* and great care must be taken to safeguard the physical well-being of all individuals!

1. The day before you plan to conduct the initiative, set up the canyon crossing swing in the following way:

   - Locate a tree that will support the weight of one person. Be very careful to select a high tree limb that will hold the heaviest participant under a dynamic load (a load in motion).

   - Make sure that there are no other obstacles in the immediate vicinity of the tree.

   - Tie the 35-foot rope over a limb of the tree and tie a foot loop approximately 15 inches in diameter at the bottom of the rope so that, under load, it is about 10 inches off the ground. Use a bowline knot, as shown in Figure 5.1.

   - The swinging rope should be long enough to allow easy mounting and dis-mounting (that is, the rope should not be more than 2 feet off the ground at the end of its swing for the heaviest participant). Test it yourself with your eyes closed to gauge the level of difficulty.

   - After you test the rope, swing once with your eyes open and note where the end of the swing is in both directions. Then, using the boards or other flat, safe objects, mark the "canyon" boundaries at the end points of your swing in each direction.

2. The day of the initiative, fill the bucket with water and place it on the side the group will start from.

3. Separate participants into two groups. Blindfold everyone in one group and ask them to go with the spirit of living without sight for the duration of this initiative.

4. Tell the other group, "I don't want to hear another sound from you for the duration of the activity" and give them Handout 5.1.

5. Instruct the sighted group to read the handout silently and to begin the activity.

6. Observe and take notes.

> *NOTE:* Only take notes if the spotting is under control. Remember that safety comes first.

7. When the team successfully completes the activity, or the time has expired, allow all participants to remove their blindfolds and debrief using the following questions:

   - How would you rate your teamwork on a scale of 1 to 10? Explain your rating.
   - What role did physical constraints play during this activity?
   - What value did you place on establishing an effective communication system?
   - What did you contribute to the success or failure of this activity?
   - Who assumed the role of the leader?
   - What incorrect assumptions did you make during this activity?
   - Did the two teams (unsighted or mute) make the most of one another's talents and resources?
   - What did you learn from this experience?
   - How can you relate what happened to your own work environment?

QUOTE

"Face your fears, and the death of fear is certain—thinking may not overcome fear, but action will."

Unknown

Figure 5.1. How to Tie a Bowline Knot

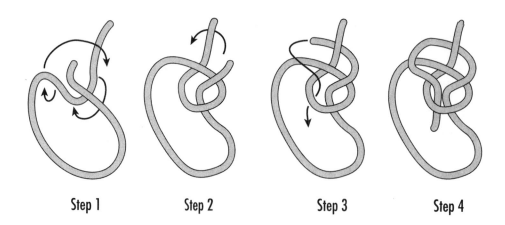

Step 1   Step 2   Step 3   Step 4

Keep the cross point in Step 1 between a finger and thumb and make a clock-wise turn with your wrist. Without the loop between, it is not the same knot. There is a rule of thumb which states that the loose end should be as long as 12 times the circumference for the sake of safety.

INSTRUCTIONS FOR CANYON OF NO RETURN

The objective of this activity is to get your whole team across the "canyon" (the area that has been marked off) *as safely and effectively as possible* using the rope swing. You are also required to transport the container of liquid across the "Canyon of No Return," spilling *none* of the liquid. You will have up to 20 minutes to complete this task.

- The restrictions on sight and speech that have been placed on your team must remain in effect until the *entire* task has been completed, that is, your entire team and the container of liquid are all safely over on the far side.

- No one may touch the area inside the boundary markers at any time. Should any-one touch inside the boundary, that person must walk around to the beginning point and start again. Anything that touches the area between the boundary boards is immediately forfeited.

- If any of the liquid is spilled at any time, the container must be refilled and then transported across the canyon again.

- No one may walk around the canyon (unless returning to begin again). Trees may not be utilized, and the boundary markers may not be moved.

- A minimum of two "spotters" must be available to receive any blindfolded individuals who are swinging across.

- No more than one person can be on the rope at one time, and only those resources you have on your person can be used.

#6 SPACE STATION LOCKOUT*

OVERVIEW

Participants are separated into two groups: "space walkers" and "space station workers." The space walkers become locked out of their space station due to an equipment malfunction. The space walkers have to assemble two cubes under significant constraints, with only nonverbal directions from the space station workers in order to re-enter the space station.

OBJECTIVES

- To demonstrate the importance of all forms of communication
- To experience team dynamics when developing a communication system
- To experience the concept of adaptability
- To experience cooperation among team members and various personality types
- To incorporate creativity into problem solving

GROUP SIZE

Twenty to thirty people in two groups

MATERIALS

- Enough blindfolds for all "space walkers"
- Six "Zoo Walls" of one color (to make one cube)+
- Six "Zoo Walls" of a different color (to make a second cube)
- Rope or yellow "caution" tape
- Trees, stakes, or fence posts (if outdoors) or chairs or tables (if indoors) to be used as corners for the marked-off area shown in Figure 6.1
- One copy of Figure 6.1
- Copies of Handout 6.1 in envelopes for the space walkers
- A method for timing the initiative

---

*This initiative was created by John Burchinal, senior facilitator at Harris Semiconductor.

+Zoo Walls are available from Learning Products Snap Wall® System products. Contact Learning Products, Inc., 700 Fee Fee Road, St. Louis, MO 63043; 888-EDU-KIDS or e-mail info@learningproducts.com. You may also want to visit the Learning Products website at (http://www.learningproducts.com/snapwall.htm).

PHYSICAL SET-UP

Either indoors or outdoors. See Figure 6.1 for the layout.

SUGGESTED TIME

120 minutes (60-minute exercise with a 60-minute debriefing)

PROCEDURE

1. Using Figure 6.1 as a guide, rope or tape off an area to identify the space where the blindfolded space walkers will be. Arrange the Zoo Wall pieces as indicated in the figure.

> NOTE: Do not allow the space walkers to see the roped-off site before they begin. You particularly do not want them to see the pieces for the cubes on the ground. If necessary, put the cube pieces down after the blindfolds are put in place.

2. Place one copy of Handout 6.1 in an envelope.

3. Identify who will be the space walkers and who will be the space station workers. Give each space walker a blindfold.

4. Instruct the space walkers to put on their blindfolds, simulating the darkness of the far side of the moon.

5. Give the envelope containing Handout 6.1 to the space station workers and ask them to read it. Meanwhile, lead the blindfolded space walkers to the roped-off area (it is recommended that space walkers hold hands, forming a human chain, during this period) and help them to enter the roped-off area. Explain to them that they are inside a confined area, describing the rope or tape and whatever is being used as corner posts.

6. Explain to the space walkers that they were on a space walk when the unthinkable happened: The hatch malfunctioned, preventing their return to the space station. The workers inside the space station can see them but cannot verbally communicate with them. Tell them that they only have a one-hour supply of oxygen in their space suits. Remind the space walkers that they are free to use any form of communication they choose to, but they must keep their blindfolds in place at all times. Leave the space walkers in the roped-off area, instructing them to remain still and quiet until the initiative begins.

7. Return to the space station workers and check to see whether they have any questions about their tasks as outlined in Handout 6.1.

8. Lead them to the space walkers' area and tell them to begin the initiative.

9. Observe and take notes for the debriefing session.

10. Upon successful completion of the exercise (or when time is up), conduct the debriefing session using the following questions:

- What problems did your team face?
- How did you handle any communication issues?
- How important a part did listening play during this activity?
- How would you rate your teamwork on a scale of 1 to 10? Why?
- What behaviors made the rescue possible?
- How can you relate this to your work environment?

VARIATION

You can instruct the space station workers to tell the space walkers to assemble the cubes by color.

QUOTE

"All too frequently, employees do good work in spite of the organization and its leadership, rather than because of them."

Alexander Lucia

Figure 6.1. Layout for Space Station Lockout

approximately 40 yards per side

INSTRUCTIONS FOR SPACE STATION LOCKOUT

Situation

You are a worker on Space Station Alpha. The entrance hatch to the station has malfunctioned, stranding a number of space walkers outside the space station. The station is currently located on the far side of the moon, where there is complete darkness. Voice communications with the space walkers has been cut off. The only means of communicating with them is through nonverbal commands. They seem to be able to hear some noises through the space station wall (clapping, foot stomping, tapping on the fence posts or chairs). You and the other space station workers must devise a signaling system for communicating with the space walkers.

The positive aspect of this situation is that you can see the space walkers. However, they cannot see you. Materials that will allow the space walkers to rebuild the entrance hatch are available to them, but they are unable to see them. They must have your help. Once the space walkers have properly assembled and connected the new space station entrance, they will be able to safely return to the secure confines of the space station. There is one more constraint: The space walkers have only a 1-hour supply of oxygen.

Your task is to nonverbally instruct the space walkers to build two cubes from the twelve Zoo Walls by snapping them together and stacking them (it is okay if the finished cubes contain walls of different colors unless they were instructed that they be built with the same color). The space walkers can then return safely through the hatch into the space station. The space walkers know they have only 1 hour.

You must remain outside the roped-off area and may not have any physical contact with the space walkers or the materials inside.

Your team has 2 minutes to discuss a plan. Once you are taken to the space station, verbal communication ceases.

#7 HUMAN WEB

OVERVIEW

The team stands in a tight circle with shoulders touching. They then reach into the circle and randomly join hands in the middle of the circle. The team's task is to untangle the web they have created without letting go of one another's hands.

OBJECTIVES

- To warm up a group of participants
- To give participants who do not know one another an opportunity to meet and work together on a fun problem-solving task

GROUP SIZE

Eight to twelve participants per "web"

MATERIALS

- Enough blindfolds for half of the participants if using Variation 2
- Enough six-inch pieces of string for each participant to have one if using Variation 3
- A method for timing the initiative

PHYSICAL SET-UP

This activity can be conducted indoors or outdoors. Space must be available for the group or groups to be able to move around.

SUGGESTED TIME

50 to 95 minutes (30-minute to 45-minute activity with 20-minute to 50-minute debriefing)

PROCEDURE

> *SAFETY REMINDER:* This activity involves bending, kneeling, stretching, and so forth. Ensure everyone's safety at all times.

1. **This** activity requires a minimum of three participants.

2. **Ask** participants to stand facing one another in a very tight circle with their shoulders touching.

3. **Instruct** participants to put their right hands into the circle and to take hold of someone else's right hand, but not the hand of the person to their immediate right or left.

4. **Instruct** participants to now put their left hands into the circle and take hold of someone else's left hand, again not the hand of the person on their immediate right or left. Tell them that they cannot take the left hand of the person whose right hand they are already holding.

5. **Tell** the group that their challenge is to untangle the human web while continuing to hold hands at all times. Adjustment of grip for safety or comfort is permitted.

6. **Have** the group continue until the knot is unraveled in the form of a large circle (or possibly two circles). If they are stuck and believe that they have a web that cannot be untangled, tell them that they have the opportunity to break *only one* grip in the group and to have that one grip reunited "outside the knot." Observe their decision-making process. (Was there consensus?)

7. **Once** a decision has been made as to which grip will be changed, let the group implement the decision and continue untying their knot.

8. **Once** the web is untangled, or the time has expired, conduct a debriefing session using the following questions:

   - What was your initial reaction when I said, "Untie the knot"?
   - Did anyone think it could not be done?
   - What was required in order to solve the problem? (possible responses include communication, decision making, experimentation, trust, etc.)
   - How effectively did the group collaborate on solving the problem?
   - In what ways do you become "tied up in knots" back in your current work environment?
   - What insights can you take back to your day-to-day job environment?

9. **If** you conduct Variation 2 (blindfolds), ask the following questions in addition to the ones already listed above:

   - What level of trust did you have with your teammates?
   - What problems arose when the group tried to untangle the web?
   - Did you feel any loss of control?

VARIATIONS

1. Challenge the group to try the activity again without talking.

2. Follow the same procedures except have every other person blindfolded.

3. Use string instead of hands. This option makes the activity easier. To utilize this variation, provide each participant with a 6-inch piece of string, which they should hold in their right hands. Have the participants put their right hands (holding the string) into the circle, and then, with their left hands, grab the end of a different piece of string, but not the string of the person to their immediate right or left. Once everyone is connected, conduct and debrief the activity as explained above.

QUOTE

"Any significant breakthrough was first started with a break with the past."

Stephen Covey

#8 TEAM POWER

OVERVIEW

The team must locate an object and return it to the group. The members have several restrictions that require them to work synergistically in order to accomplish their goal. Powerful!

OBJECTIVES

- To demonstrate metaphorically how important each team member's contribution is to team power
- To demonstrate the need for everyone to work together
- To establish an effective communication process critical to success of the team

GROUP SIZE

One to four teams of four members each

MATERIALS

- Three bandannas for each team
- An object for each team to locate (a Koosh® ball works well)
- A method for timing the initiative

PHYSICAL SET-UP

Indoors or outdoors

SUGGESTED TIME

75 to 90 minutes (30-minute activity with a 45-minute to 60-minute debriefing)

PROCEDURE

1. Prior to the activity, choose the area you plan to use for this initiative. The size of the area required is dependent on the number of teams participating. Each team

must be free to move around **without** restriction from other teams. The area must be free of obstructions. If **you are conducting** this activity outdoors, make sure the area you plan to use is dry so **that participants** do not get their clothes wet.

2. Separate the participants into **four-pers**on teams and have each team sit in a circle.

3. Have each team identify persons **1, 2, 3**, and 4 and instruct them as follows:

   Person 1 cannot speak, can **move, and** cannot see.

   Person 2 cannot speak, cannot **move, and** cannot see.

   Person 3 cannot speak, cannot **move, and** can see.

   Person 4 can speak, cannot **move, and** cannot see.

   > NOTE: "Cannot move" **means that** the person must sit in one place, but is able to gesture.

4. Give out the bandannas and **tell the thr**ee members of each team who cannot **see** to blindfold themselves.

5. Tell the teams that their objective **is to** locate an object that has been laid outside their circle and to **return it to the circle**. They must follow the rules exactly. The **time** constraint is 30 minutes.

6. Observe and take notes for the **debriefin**g. When facilitating several teams, ensure that teams who have located **their object** stay quiet while the others finish. It is highly unlikely that all **teams will finish** at the same time. In fact, it is possible that no team will locate and **return the object**.

7. After all teams have returned **their obje**cts, or the time has expired, conduct a debriefing session using **the following** questions:

   - How successful were you in **finding** the object?
   - What difficulties did you **experience?**
   - How did the member who was **unable** to speak, see, or walk feel about this exercise? In what ways does **this mirror** actual team experiences?
   - What emotions did you **experience in** your role?
   - Please share your feelings **about this** activity.
   - What type of communication **system** did your team establish?
   - How successful was the **communicat**ion system on your team? Explain.
   - How did the person able to **speak fee**l about having the entire team relying on him or her?
   - What did you learn about **teamwork** from this activity?
   - How can you apply the knowledge **g**ained from this experience in your work environment?

QUOTE

*"The most important thing in **communi**cation is hearing what isn't being said."*

Peter F. Drucker

#9 YELLOW GOOEY STICKY MESS*

OVERVIEW

"When you go from being a caterpillar to becoming a butterfly, you're nothing more than a yellow gooey sticky mess" is how Ted Forbes talked about issues involving individual and organizational change; it is about a transformation and structure. You also must stop being one thing in order to become something different.

This is an interactive activity supported with a few great quotes—a hands-on activity and an easy process to engage participants in considering change.

OBJECTIVES

- To generate an interactive and kinesthetic learning event that is simple, low in cost, and quite memorable
- To build an environment for discussing issues surrounding personal, team, and organizational transformation

GROUP SIZE

Any number of participants grouped into teams of five to six members each

MATERIALS

- Transparencies or flip charts with the following quotes:

  "When you go from being a caterpillar to becoming a butterfly, you're nothing more than a yellow, gooey, sticky mess."

  "It is dangerous to know THE answer."

  "Even caterpillars. . . ."

- Handout 9.1 for the facilitator

---

*This initiative is from Dr. Scott Simmerman, managing partner of Performance Management Company in Taylors, South Carolina. This story has formed the basis of a series of illustrations and metaphors by the author and a program called "Square Wheels: Teaching the Caterpillar to Fly" that has been delivered at conferences and seminars worldwide. The Gack Recipe, along with others and an article of the same name, can be found in the resources section of Dr. Simmerman's website: www.squarewheels.com.

- Materials for making Gack as described on Handout 9.2
- Newsprint or butcher paper to protect tabletops

PHYSICAL SET-UP
Tables for each group

SUGGESTED TIME
45 minutes (15-minute activity with a 30-minute debriefing)

PROCEDURE

1. Start with an introduction explaining the purpose of the meeting and the focus on change and transformation.

2. Tell the following joke in an animated way:

   "Two caterpillars were walking along when a beautiful butterfly floated by. The one caterpillar said to the other: 'You'll never get me up in one of those things.'"

   (You may choose to illustrate this joke with a colorful drawing or picture of a butterfly.)

3. Ask participants for a show of hands as to how many understood the joke. Ask everyone to discuss the joke for two minutes among themselves in small groups.

4. At the completion of the two minutes, ask them for the key ideas and main learning point. (Many potential answers are possible, including fear of flying, resistance to change, the potential already exists, and my personal favorite: "My mother was a moth.")

5. Present the following transparency or flip-chart sheet: "It is dangerous to know THE answer."

6. While showing the quote, make the comment that "THE" is pronounced "Duh," and that by knowing the answer, we close ourselves off to considering other possibilities. Say that there is generally more than one answer and that knowing an old solution may get in the way of thinking about new ones. Tell participants that is not a smart nor effective thing to do. We must always be open for new ideas from those around us.

7. At this point, read Handout 9.1 to everyone.

8. Now tell the group that a friend recently called to ask if you knew anything about caterpillars and butterflies. Prompt the group with your voice and a gesture to respond audibly: "So I said . . .?" The group, even after just learning that it is dangerous to know the answer and not consider other possibilities, is easily prompted to fill in the answer, "Yes." Ask the question again, indicating that they should reconsider their answer. They should discover, after a minute or two, that the best answer is "No."

9. Then say, "Right! So, I answer 'no' and my friend says" (show the following quote as a transparency or on a flip chart):

   "When you go from being a caterpillar to becoming a butterfly, you're nothing more than a yellow gooey sticky mess."

10. (Optional) At this point, you can inject an active learning event—the making of a hands-on gooey mess. The concoction starts out as two containers of watery substances and ends up as a gooey colloidal suspension commonly called Gack. You can make one large "demo" unit and pass around samples or you can have each table make a batch. Follow the instructions on Handout 9.2.

11. There are a lot of ways to continue to build on the metaphor, depending on your personal style and your learning objectives. End with a message about leadership and the need for constant and positive communication within the work group.

12. Present the "Even caterpillars" transparency or flip chart and allow the participants to suggest ways to complete the sentence. The complete quote is "Even caterpillars can fly if they would just lighten up!"

13. Debrief using the following questions:

    • How does the butterfly metaphor relate to change within an organization?

    • Does it relate more to personal or organizational change? Explain.

    • What (besides more than you probably ever thought you would learn about caterpillars) did you learn from this activity?

    • How does the "yellow gooey sticky mess" metaphor apply to organizational and/or personal change?

    • What can we learn from the caterpillar?

QUOTE

"Follow your dreams, for as you dream, so shall you become."

Unknown

YELLOW GOOEY STICKY MESS FACTS ABOUT BUTTERFLIES AND MOTHS

- There are more than 142,000 species of moths and about 20,000 species of butterflies.

- Moths have feathery antenna. Butterflies have sensors on the end of a stalk.

- Moths generally have fuzzy bodies.

- Moths generally fly only at night, butterflies mostly in daylight.

- Both have six legs and two sets of wings.

- Butterflies fold up their wings when they are at rest; moths generally leave theirs unfolded.

- Some caterpillars eat as much as 27,000 times their body weight to support their transition into flying insects.

- Butterflies and moths start out as eggs. These hatch into caterpillars, which go through a pupa or metamorphosis stage and then evolve into the winged version. The cycle can take as little as 3 weeks in the tropics and many months in colder climes. Cold-climate species can hibernate for as long as 9 months.

- Butterflies mate, end to end, facing in different directions while they are in flight. Mating can last from 20 minutes to several hours!

- Caterpillars shed their skins. As the insect becomes too large for its body, the skin splits and the caterpillar crawls out wearing a new stretchy skin. This can happen several times before metamorphosis. Change is thus not unknown even to caterpillars!

- The adult butterfly or moth does not grow, while the caterpillar increases in size many times.

- Goat moth caterpillars can take 3 or 4 years to mature!

- Butterflies will fight for control of a sunny spot! But they are not tough enough to hurt each other.

- The solitary Oak Leaf Miner has wings that span less than a quarter of an inch. The Two-Tailed Swallowtail Butterfly and Cecropia Moth have wingspans in excess of 6 inches, and some tropical butterflies like the Queen Alexandra from New Guinea have spans of more than 11 inches.

- The Monarch butterfly can fly at up to 20 miles per hour and can migrate more than 80 miles per day. Some Monarchs from Canada migrate to Mexico, a distance of more than 2,000 miles.

- The big green adult Luna Moths lack a mouth and actually live only on the energy stored during their larval stage. The sole focus of their adult lives is reproduction. The male can sense a female as far as 5 miles away.

YELLOW GOOEY STICK MESS RECIPE FOR GACK

Mix the following items together:

- 2 cups of milk-based white glue
- 1½ cups warm water
- yellow food coloring as desired
- 1½ tablespoons Borax
- 1 cup water

You can use one large container to mix the gack and then provide samples in clear plastic cups for each group, or each group can mix up a smaller batch in clear plastic cups.

> *NOTE:* The Gack sticks to cloth and it is also not a good idea to put it on any fine finish such as a hardwood conference table!

#10 TRUST WALK

OVERVIEW

One member of a pair is blindfolded and led along a predetermined route by a fellow team member. This works well when team members are not communicating or do not know one another very well. There are many eye-opening dynamics relating to communication and the concept of trust in this activity.

OBJECTIVES

- To provide a simple way to demonstrate the dynamics of trust, communication, and interrelating
- To allow for flexibility and creativity of all those involved
- To develop teamwork and synergy

GROUP SIZE

Any even number of participants between two and thirty with a ratio of one facilitator to ten participants

MATERIALS

- Blindfolds for half the participants

PHYSICAL SET-UP

Indoors

SUGGESTED TIME

60 to 75 minutes (30-minute activity with a 30-minute to 45-minute debriefing)

PROCEDURE

1. Prior to the activity, choose the route the group will traverse.

   - Make it interesting and challenging.

   - Double check the path you plan to use for potential safety hazards.

   - There is no need to select a hazardous route, as wearing a blindfold creates the perception of danger by itself.

   - The route can be as simple as walking down some hallways, then returning to the starting point. Blindfolded, that in itself is quite an experience.

2. Separate participants into pairs. Allow pairs to choose which person will be blindfolded and which will be the guide. Each blindfolded participant will be guided by his or her partner. This will require communication and trust by both participants.

3. Tell each pair to blindfold the chosen person.

4. Show the selected route to the guides.

5. Have the pairs traverse your pre-planned route.

6. Keep an eye on the group for safety's sake. Take mental notes about group actions, comments, and behaviors that you can use during the debriefing session.

7. Conduct a debriefing session using the following questions:

   - How did team members who were blindfolded feel?

   - As a guide, what did you feel?

   - How well did your pair communicate?

   - Was communication different as a result of the circumstances? Explain.

   - What difficulties did you experience?

   - What can you learn from this experience?

   - In what ways does this experience parallel your current work environment?

   - What insights can you take back to your day-to-day job environment?

QUOTE

"There is very little difference in people. But that little difference makes a big difference. The little difference is attitude. The big difference is whether it is positive or negative."

W. Clement Stone

#11 TRUST ME

OVERVIEW

Teammates use specific commands to ensure safety while one individual trusts another to catch him or her as he or she falls backward.

OBJECTIVES

- To develop trust between teammates
- To allow participants to practice spotting and verbal commands
- To develop communication skills between teammates

GROUP SIZE

This activity can be done with any number of participants. However, it is wise to maintain a facilitator ratio of 1 per 12 participants. An even number of participants is desired, but if an odd number exists, individuals may take turns so that everyone has a chance to participate.

MATERIALS

None

PHYSICAL SET-UP

An open area with ample space, either indoors (a carpeted area is best, for safety reasons) or outdoors (a grassy area, for safety reasons)

SUGGESTED TIME

60 minutes (30-minute activity with a 30-minute debriefing)

PROCEDURE

1. Ask participants to form pairs. Stress to participants that partners, for safety reasons, should be of equal size and weight.

2. Tell each pair to select one member to be the "faller" and the other to be the "spotter." Explain that partners will later switch roles.

3. Inform the participants of the commands they must use to ensure safety. Write them on a flip chart or board and have them practice the following:

   Faller says: "Faller ready."

   Spotter says: "Spotter ready."

   Faller says: "Ready to fall."

   Spotter says: "Fall on."

4. Demonstrate the proper method for catching the falling team members: legs about shoulder width apart, one foot behind the other, legs bent, hands palm up, elbows bent at about chest height.

5. Tell the faller to stand at arm's length in front of the spotter and to then turn his or her back to the spotter.

6. Tell the participants they may begin the activity once they are in place.

7. Ask participants to switch roles and repeat the task.

8. Conduct a debriefing session using the following questions:

   - What role did trust play in this initiative?
   - Did you develop trust in your teammates?
   - What contributes to the development of trust between team members?
   - In what ways does this activity parallel your current work environment?
   - What insights can you take back to your day-to-day job environment?

QUOTE

"No matter how trifling the matter at hand, do it with a feeling that it demands the best that is in you."

Sir William Osler

#12 THE SWORD IN THE STONE TEAM CHALLENGE

OVERVIEW

This initiative provides a unique team experience that requires a combination of creativity, critical thinking, breaking through perceived barriers, and good group dynamics. The team is presented with a challenge: to remove a model sword from a frame ("the stone").

OBJECTIVES

- To provide a challenging task that requires processing data and ideas from team members
- To demonstrate that teamwork has tremendous benefits for solving complex problems
- To build trust and team relationships
- To highlight dysfunctional team behaviors while enhancing positive problem-solving behaviors

GROUP SIZE

Four to twenty-four people, divided into teams of four members each (although larger teams will also work)

MATERIALS

- One Sword in the Stone puzzle* for each team
- One copy of Handouts 12.1, 12.2, 12.3, and 12.4 for each team+
- One Sword in the Stone Background Information Sheet for the facilitator
- A method for timing the initiative

_____

*The Sword in the Stone puzzle with handouts can be purchased from *www.EdRose.com* or by calling 407-254-1495.

+Handouts 12.2, 12.3, and 12.4 (the clues to the puzzle) and the Background Information Sheet are included with the puzzle.

PHYSICAL SET-UP

Indoors with tables for teams to work through the puzzle

SUGGESTED TIME

90 minutes (60 minutes for the puzzle, with 30 minutes for debriefing)

> *NOTE:* The clues and handouts required to solve the mystery are included with each puzzle. In addition to the team handouts, a copy of complete instructions for solving the mystery are included to ensure your complete understanding of the puzzle before using it with teams. Attempt to solve it yourself before looking at the solution or trying it with a team. Another option is to take a small team and work through the mystery with them. The value of self-discovery learning that you can produce with this initiative is well worth your time and effort. The benefit of using this activity is the 20 years of history behind it and the data collected on teams that have solved it. In addition, it introduces the concept of keeping a secret, subsequently building trusting team relationships.

PROCEDURE

1. Prior to conducting this activity, familiarize yourself with the contents of Handout 12.1 and with the debriefing questions.

2. Separate the group into teams of four to ten members each.

3. Inform everyone that they will be participating in a unique activity, a challenge that has been attempted by over 30,000 people (as of June 14, 1998) and solved by only 937. The shortest time on record for an individual to solve the puzzle was 45 minutes, and the longest was one year.

4. Tell the team that when they successfully solve the puzzle they will be eligible for membership in The International Teamwork Society's "Who's Who," an organization for the advancement of world teamwork. Explain that The International Teamwork Society is based on King Arthur's Round Table concept. King Arthur seated his knights at a round table, and he too functioned as a team member. All were equal participants in solving the problems presented to the group. The heroics and expertise of each member were tested and valued. Each performed leadership roles when needed, but all remained teammates throughout.

5. Tell the groups to solve the mystery as quickly as possible, but that they will have 60 minutes to complete it if necessary.

6. Give one Sword in the Stone puzzle to each team. (You may give out more than one puzzle per team if you wish, but this could cause teams to lose focus.)

7. Give one copy of Handout 12.1 to each team (or you may give one copy to each team member) and have one person per group read the handout aloud to the entire team.

8. Tell the teams to begin.

9. Provide clues as requested by the teams. Track the costs from Handout 12.1 for each clue you give.

> NOTE: You can ensure that everyone succeeds, if that is your goal. If a team is having problems, go over and say that you are a consultant and have some experience in this area and would like to share it with them. Don't do the work for them, but ask the right questions so that they will arrive at the right answers themselves. Naturally, you will have to know how to solve the puzzle yourself and be very familiar with the process.

10. Take notes, by team, for the debriefing session.

11. After the teams have completed the puzzle (or 60 minutes have expired), conduct a debriefing session using questions based on the outcome.

12. If a team has successfully solved the puzzle, shake each member's hand and welcome them into the "Who's Who," an order dedicated to improving teamwork around the world. Tell them that they have now become "Keepers of the Secret."

> NOTE: If one of the groups solves the puzzle when others do not, use the concept of benchmarking or networking to allow them to share their knowledge. Have them present their information in such a way that other teams will learn for themselves how the puzzle is solved.

13a. (Successful Completion) Debrief using the following questions after successful completion of the puzzle:

- What contributed to your success?
- How much importance did you place on the time and number of stones?
- Was it more important to remove the sword or to watch the costs?
- What was your team's strategy, if you had one?
- Were you motivated by the fact that few people have solved the puzzle?
- What was the single most important team behavior that contributed to your solving the mystery?
- The cost was in stones. What does that mean? Did you apply more real value to the stones than you should have? Is there an analogy to be drawn with your behavior in real life?
- Did you experience any of the following in completing the task: Adaptability? Trustworthiness? Resourcefulness? Optimism? Consideration?
- What did you learn from this experience? How can what you have learned be applied to your current work environment?

13b. (Unsuccessful Completion) Ask the following questions for unsuccessful completion:

- What problems did you face as a team?
- Did you effectively process the clues?

The Sword in the Stone Team Challenge

- What value did you place on the stones?
- Just exactly how much value does a stone have? Did you tend to place your own meanings or values on them? How is this comparable to how people act in real life?
- Was your goal to remove the sword at all costs?
- Did the language of the clues throw you off? In what way?
- If the clues had been written differently, do you think that would have helped you to solve the puzzle? In what way?

14. If teams want to continue to work on the puzzle, allow them to if possible, being sure to let them know how to reach you for discussion.

SWORD IN THE STONE BACKGROUND INFORMATION

This initiative is a simulation of the 12th century legend of King Arthur and has some intriguing aspects to it. The Challenge was created by Jim Hand of Laramie, Wyoming, in 1976, and to date some 30,000 have been sold. Only 937, or 3 percent, of those trying on their own have registered as having solved the mystery as of this writing. I was the 937th person to solve the mystery, and it took me almost five hours doing it by myself.

The mystery is very difficult for an individual to solve because the human mind has a very hard time with the steps required to solve the problem. The clues are so complex and put together so well that an individual must have the patience of Job to go through each and every clue.

However, if a team processes all the information (clues) effectively, the team can solve it in record time. Since turning this into a team initiative, we have had 11 of 12 teams be successful, a success rate of 92 percent, versus an individual success rate of just 3 percent. The first three groups we used it with had the following results: Within 15 minutes the first team had asked for all the clues, and they solved the problem in 46 minutes. The second team asked for the first of the clues after 15 minutes and the second and third clues after 40 minutes; they completed the puzzle in 48 minutes. The last team asked for the first clue after 45 minutes and then the second clue shortly thereafter; however, they were never able to solve the puzzle on their own. I asked one of the other team members to see whether they wanted any help, which they did. This is the kind of behavior we want to reinforce. We want people to ask for help and to utilize resources to solve problems. It also is a metaphor for different groups helping one another in solving problems.

The team success rate will be updated on my web site, *www.EdRose.com.* Please send your results to erose@harris.com.

The key to solving this problem as a team is in processing all available clues and using the team's collective intellect. This hands-on, synergistic activity has the unique ability to build trust between team members because they are required to keep the secret of the sword. The initiative can demonstrate powerful learning outcomes for the participants.

THE SWORD IN THE STONE TEAM CHALLENGE

Teamwork is about working together to accomplish things we never thought possible alone. A 12th-century situation has been updated to test your team's creativity and problem-solving abilities. Your team will face a unique challenge: to remove a sword from a stone.

Those who solve the puzzle become members of an elite group.

Removing the sword from the stone creates a strong bond between team members, because you will have solved a problem together that very few people have solved alone.

Team members will share a closely guarded secret that should be discussed with no one who has not solved the mystery. They will become members of the International Teamwork Society's "Who's Who," continuing to work on the following sacred behaviors, used for thousands of years by the most successful people: *adaptability, trustworthiness, resourcefulness, optimism,* and *consideration.* These must become watchwords for your team. The Society simply refers to these behaviors as *ATROC.* Members will receive recognition as skilled problem solvers and will be encouraged to use the *ATROC* behaviors in their daily lives, promoting their well-being and the success of their teams.

Team Task

Your team challenge is to remove the sword from the stone and replace it while the facilitator watches. Time constraints will be given by the facilitator. Three clues are available. You are free to ask for clues as needed; however, each team must keep a record of the time taken and the number of clues requested. Clues are valued in stones according to the following chart:

1st Clue = 10 Stones

2nd Clue = 20 Stones

3rd Clue = 20 Stones

Success is determined by your ability to remove the sword from the stone and to replace it correctly. Teams must do the following to the facilitator's satisfaction:

1. Show that the sword is bound according to the picture.

2. Demonstrate unbinding the sword.

3. Rebind the sword as it was originally.

4. Agree to keep the secret!

Bound

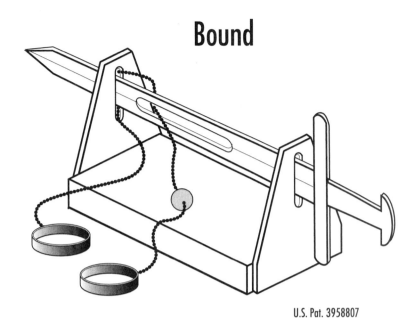

U.S. Pat. 3958807

Freed

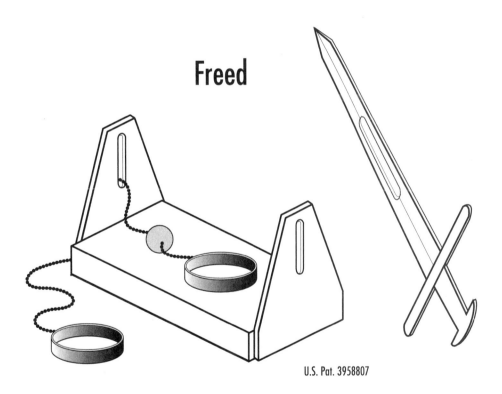

U.S. Pat. 3958807

#13   WILLOW TREE

OVERVIEW

One participant stands in the middle of the group with arms folded and eyes closed. On command, the person falls backward into a spotter's hands and is freely passed from person to person around the circle.

OBJECTIVES

- To identify various levels of trust between participants
- To provide a fun way to evaluate the dynamic of trust among team members
- To warm up the group or lead into more complex initiatives

GROUP SIZE

Eight to twelve participants per circle with an unlimited number of circles

MATERIALS

- Blindfolds (one per circle, if using the variation)
- A flip chart and markers

PHYSICAL SET-UP

Indoors or out, with enough room to accommodate all circles. The space should allow for movement and be carpeted or grassy.

SUGGESTED TIME

60 minutes (30-minute activity with a 30-minute debriefing)

PROCEDURE

1. Divide the participants into groups of eight to twelve participants each.

2. Instruct each group to stand and form a circle.

3. Ask for a volunteer from each group to enter their circle and stand equidistant from other participants, who should be able to extend their arms and touch this person.

4. Instruct the volunteers to stand with their arms folded across their chests, their eyes closed, and their legs tight together—"so tight that you can hold a quarter between them."

5. Instruct the participants who are forming the circle to put their hands up in front of them with palms outward and upward. Explain that they will need to catch and cushion the person in the center when he or she falls.

6. Instruct the participants to use the following commands, writing them on a board or flip chart:
   - Person inside the circle says, "Faller ready."
   - People forming the circle say, "Spotters ready."
   - Person falling says, "Ready to fall."
   - People forming the circle say, "Fall on."

7. The person falls backward.

8. Each group then pushes the falling team member around within the circle as they wish.

9. Allow the groups to push the person around for approximately 1 minute (you want the faller to become comfortable with being supported by the team members).

10. Conduct a debriefing session using the following questions:
    - What did you experience as the member in the middle?
    - How does this relate to teamwork? Do team members in the real world support one another?
    - In what ways does this activity parallel your current work environment?
    - What insights can you take back to your day-to-day job environment?

VARIATION

The person inside the circle may be blindfolded.

QUOTE

"You don't buy trust, you earn it."
Unknown

#14 HOW MANY BALLS CAN YOU JUGGLE?

OVERVIEW

Participants are asked to juggle balls (a metaphor for jobs or team tasks), and when problems occur their reactions to these problems become the focus of the debriefing session. Participants realize that it is often not what someone says that is the problem, but how feelings are shown through nonverbal actions.

OBJECTIVES

- To see how individuals adapt to working together under stress
- To create an environment in which participants see how interpersonal relationships can deteriorate as a result of even the smallest nonverbal actions
- To demonstrate how important and influential nonverbal clues are to the person receiving the information

GROUP SIZE

Six to twenty participants

MATERIALS

- One ball per participant minus one, for example, nineteen balls for twenty people. Koosh® balls, whiffle balls, or tennis balls work best. For issues of safety, the softer and lighter the ball, the better.

PHYSICAL SET-UP

Enough space so that participants can juggle (throw) objects

SUGGESTED TIME

75 minutes (30-minute activity with 45-minute debriefing)

PROCEDURE

1. Have the participants form a circle and tell them you are going to have them juggle some balls.

2. Tell the group that "quality," in the context of this activity, means the speed with which they juggle and how well they are able to keep the balls in motion without any hitting the ground. ("Juggling," in this context, means keeping the balls in the air and/or in motion continuously within the group.)

3. Give one of the participants one ball. Instruct him or her to toss the ball to another participant and for that participant to toss it to another, and so on. Let the participants get used to the process.

4. Add additional balls as you see fit. See how many the group can handle.

5. Tell the participants that often at work they will be required to juggle many jobs or tasks at once. Explain that the balls in this activity serve as metaphors for those jobs or tasks and that the team's objective is to juggle as many balls (jobs or tasks) as possible.

6. Keep the "juggling" going for awhile. Base your decision to stop the activity on the energy or interest level of the group. When you see the group's energy decreasing (or when several people lose interest), end the activity.

7. An option at this point is to ask the group to meet together for a few minutes to determine ways to improve its results.

8. If the option in Step 7 is chosen, let the participants try the initiative again using their ideas.

9. Conduct a debriefing session using the following questions:
   - How would you rate your teamwork during this activity on a scale of 1 to 10, with 10 being high? Explain your rating.
   - What were your feelings toward members who dropped the balls? Were you angry? Upset? Thinking that person should be fired?
   - What other emotions did you feel?
   - Is there a customer/supplier analogy that could be drawn? What issues did you experience with your "customer" or "supplier"?
   - Think of the balls as jobs or tasks that your team was required to complete. In this kind of situation, how can the team members ensure success?
   - What changes would you make to improve your teamwork?
   - What could you do to improve the process? (If this was not covered in Steps 7 and 8 above. Some possible answers for this question include making eye contact before delivering the ball and/or calling out the other person's name before throwing a ball.)
   - In what ways was this activity similar to your current work environment?
   - What insights can you take back to your day-to-day job environment?

QUOTE

"The leader's task, then, is to create an environment that is conducive to self-motivation."

Nido Qubein

#15 BREAKTHROUGH THINKING

OVERVIEW

Teams use established methods of "throw and catch" to meet company demands. They set goals for their performance and try to meet them. Then the facilitator challenges the groups to develop a new process and to reach a world class standard using the new process, which requires breakthrough thinking.

OBJECTIVES

- To use creative methods to solve problems
- To accept changes that promote learning
- To experience the concept of breakthrough thinking
- To allow participants to experience continuous improvement

GROUP SIZE

Six to twelve participants per team

MATERIALS

- Four tennis or Koosh® balls per team
- A flip chart and easel
- Felt-tipped markers
- A method for timing the initiative

PHYSICAL SET-UP

Enough space to accommodate the number of teams and to allow them to conduct the activity without disturbing one another

SUGGESTED TIME

75 to 90 minutes (30-minute activity with a 45-minute to 60-minute debriefing)

PROCEDURE

1. Tell the participants that they now work for the Throw & Catch Company.

2. Give the following rules to participants:

   - Each team will form a circle.

   - Each participant will raise the hand he or she catches with and will keep it raised at all times, except to catch a ball.

   - The participant who first receives a ball will throw it to someone else and remember who that person is. Each person will always throw the ball to the same person. When the first person who threw the ball receives it again, he or she will throw it to me, which will end the process.

3. Form the participants into teams of six to twelve each and ask each team to form a circle.

4. Begin by giving a ball to one member of each team.

5. Instruct the teams to begin.

6. Introduce the other three balls, one at a time, into the process for each team. Allow each team to practice the process.

7. After the teams have had an opportunity to practice and all four balls have been returned to you, tell the teams that you will now begin timing the process. The timing will begin when you hand the first ball to someone in the circle and will end when you receive the fourth ball back from that person.

8. Ask for a volunteer, or select one of the teams to go first.

9. Hand the first ball to one of the participants and instruct the team to begin.

10. After each team completes the task, write its time on a flip chart.

11. After all of the teams have completed the task, ask each to develop a goal for improvement by choosing a lower time in which to complete the task.

12. After each team has set a new goal, write the goal on the flip chart and instruct the teams to start the task again, still abiding by the rules in Step 2. Time each team and write the new times on the flip chart.

13. After all of the teams have completed the task for the second time, inform them that the world class time for processing four balls is 4 seconds. Tell them that this is their new goal. (The objective is to stimulate out-of-the-box thinking.) Tell the teams that they have a few minutes in which to reconsider their process.

14. Repeat the process until each team can complete the task in 4 seconds or less.

15. Conduct a debriefing session using the following questions:
    - Did your group use a leader?
    - How did your group decide on a process?
    - Did your team break any old paradigms?
    - When did the breakthrough thinking occur?
    - What contributed to your team's success?
    - In what ways does what happened parallel your current work environment?
    - What insights can you take back to your day-to-day job environment?

> *NOTE:* There are many solutions to this activity. The key is breaking out of the "throw and catch" paradigm. The participants just have to touch the ball in the predefined order, so the person initially receiving the balls could hold all four of them, go around the circle, and touch the others' hands with them.

QUOTE

"You cannot become world class using the same old paradigms of "throw and catch"; you must have and use breakthrough thinking."

Author

#16 THE ACME MINING COMPANY

OVERVIEW

Using only the materials provided, participants must pick up a tennis ball and move it from Point A to Point B without dropping it. This requires all team members to work together in unison.

OBJECTIVES

- To maximize communication skills
- To build an understanding of teamwork
- To teach creative problem solving
- To practice resourcefulness
- To illustrate the relationship between managers and employees

GROUP SIZE

- A minimum of seven people (six workers and one manager) per team
- A maximum of thirteen people (six workers, six managers, and one senior manager) per team
- Six workers are required per team, but the number of managers can fluctuate
- If there are more than thirteen people, use the extras as observers or spotters

MATERIALS

- One tennis ball
- One ring approximately 2 inches in diameter (see Figure 16.1)
- Six pieces of string or twine 15 feet in length, tied to the ring (see Figure 16.1)
- Six blindfolds (optional)
- A method for timing the initiative
- One copy of Handout 16.1 for each manager

PHYSICAL SET-UP

Indoors or outdoors

SUGGESTED TIME

50 to 60 minutes (20-minute or 30-minute activity with a 30-minute debriefing), depending on the distance and obstacles (trees, fences, doorways, steps) between Point A and Point B

PROCEDURE

1. Prior to this activity, prepare the carrying sling as shown in Figure 16.1 and lay it on the ground or floor with the ball on it (this will be Point A).

2. Select Point B and mark it somehow. The distance between Point A and Point B will vary according to the obstacles in the path between them.

3. Divide the participants into teams and either appoint the manager(s) for a team or have the team select them. (Optional) Blindfold the six workers.

> *NOTE:* Do not use the blindfold option until you have run this initiative a few times and are comfortable with it. If all six workers are blindfolded, you will need six managers; if blindfolds are not used, you will need only one manager.

4. Greet the group by saying, "Welcome to the Acme Mining Company. Unfortunately, there has been a terrible rock slide that has blocked our Number 7 mine shaft. You have been hired to do some very important work for us. Your manager will fill you in on the details."

5. Give each manager a copy of Handout 16.1. Be sure to tell them that *managers cannot physically assist workers in any way!*

6. Tell managers that when they are through planning with their workers, they may begin the activity.

7. Observe and time the activity, subtracting 4 minutes for each dropped ball. Take notes about the process for the debriefing.

8. Let the group know when there are 15, 10, and 5 minutes left.

9. A team is successful when the C4 (the tennis ball) is set in the Point B drop-off zone and the pick-up device has been removed. Allow the group to celebrate if successful.

10. Debrief using the following questions:

- (Workers) How was your relationship with management?
- (Workers) How satisfied were you with the way you were led?
- (Workers) Were you good workers?
- (Workers) What interfered with your ability to listen? What did you do to overcome the interference?
- (Workers) Did any of you think of shortening the ropes? Did you share the idea with management? Why or why not?
- (Workers) Did management freely share information with you?
- (Managers) How satisfied were you with the way your workers listened and followed your instructions?
- (Managers) Did you think of shortening the ropes? Did any workers suggest this? Did you follow their suggestions?
- In what ways does this activity parallel your current work environment?
- What insights can you take back to your day-to-day job environment?

QUOTE

"Meetings are indispensable if you don't want to do anything."
John Kenneth Galbraith

Figure 16.1. Set-Up for Point B

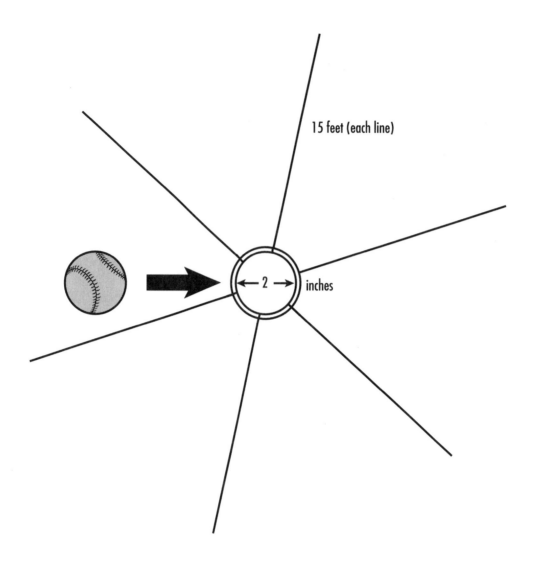

THE ACME MINING COMPANY TASK SHEET

There has been a terrible rock slide in the Number 7 shaft of the Acme Mining Company, and your team has been hired to carry C4 (plastic explosives, represented by the tennis ball) to the site so it can be used to clear away the slide.

As managers you must instruct your workers to move the C4 with a rope device and place it on Point B. However, *managers may not physically assist workers in any way.* When you have finished planning, you must position your workers at the ends of the rope handles and lead your workers through the activity.

If the C4 falls to the ground, it is rendered unstable, and your group must wait 4 minutes for it to stabilize. (There is no need to stop, as 4 minutes will be added to your finish time or 4 minutes subtracted from the 30 minutes allotted.) The team must place the ball back on the ring and start again from wherever they are. The transfer is complete when the C4 is set in the Point B drop-off zone and the rope device is removed.

You have 30 minutes to complete this process.

#17 HUNT FOR THE KEY WORD

OVERVIEW

Each group attempts to retrieve a message from a bottle in a body of water and another message from a cylinder buried in an underground location. The messages contain information that will help solve pre-assigned key questions.

OBJECTIVES

- To experience team problem solving
- To experience team competition
- To learn when to use creative thinking
- To see the impact of time constraints
- To experience collaboration

GROUP SIZE

Two groups of twelve to twenty-four participants each

MATERIALS

- Two quart-size bottles or the equivalent
- Two 2-foot cylinders with a small hole in the top (through which the team will have to retrieve the message)
- Two 100-foot lengths of rope
- Two small wooden dowel rods (about 6 inches long)
- Two 8-foot bamboo fishing poles or their equivalent
- Copies of Handouts 17.1 and 17.4 for each group
- One copy each of Handouts 17.2A, 17.2B, 17.3A, and 17.3B
- A method for timing the initiative

PHYSICAL SET-UP

Select a location outdoors, near a body of water such as a lake, pond, or pool

SUGGESTED TIME

75 to 90 minutes (45-minute to 60-minute activity with a 30-minute debriefing)

PROCEDURE

1. Prior to conducting this activity, make the following preparations:

   - Into a bottle designated for Group A, place Handout 17.2A. Into a bottle designated for Group B, place Handout 17.2B. Place the sealed bottles in the body of water.

   - Into the cylinder designated for Group A, place Handout 17.3A. Into the cylinder designated for Group B, place Handout 17.3B. Bury the cylinders to within 2 inches of their tops, with the small hole up.

   - Select the hiding place for the "key word" (Handout 17.4) and place two copies there.

2. Have the participants from into two groups of roughly equal size, A and B, using any criteria they like.

   > NOTE: Do not specifically say that they are two different teams. They will likely assume this is the case; however, the task can only be completed if both groups work together.

3. Designate two different areas around the body of water, one for each group. (Be sure each group is nearest its respective bottle and cylinder.) The two groups should be within sight of each other, but not so close that they can overhear each other.

4. Provide each group with the following materials:

   - A copy of Handout 17.1
   - One length of 100-foot rope
   - One 6-inch dowel rod
   - One 8-foot pole

5. Tell the groups that you will lead each of them to their own locations, at which time they can read Handout 17.1 and begin the activity.

6. Lead each group to its separate location and have the groups begin. Time the activity and call it to an end after 45 minutes, even if the groups have not found the key word.

   > NOTE: The trick to this activity is that each group has the answers to the other group's questions, so cooperation between the groups is imperative.

7. When one or the other (or both) of the groups comes to you with the answers to their questions:
   - Verify that their answers are correct. (If not, have them continue their deliberations.)
   - Provide them with a clue as to where they can find the key word (Handout 17.4).

8. After each group has found the key word, or time has expired, conduct a debriefing. The debriefing should focus on the process each group used. Highlight the importance of working together. Discuss that when you separate the group into two separate groups, you simulate how employees are separated by various organizational structures within a company. The following questions may be used to help guide the debriefing:
   - How did you feel about separating the group into two separate groups?
   - Were the instructions clear?
   - How successful was your group?
   - Was there a group leader? If so, who and why?
   - What obstacles did your group encounter during the initiative?
   - How was communication established between the two groups?
   - If the two groups did not work together, explain why.
   - Do these types of situations exist in the real business world?
   - What process would you do differently if you had this initiative to do over?
   - What have you learned that you can use in your own work situation?

QUOTE

"Keep on trying; often it's the last key that opens the door."
Unknown

HUNT FOR THE KEY WORD TASK SHEET

Your group has been assigned to look for the "key word." Use the following instructions to find the word:

1. A message is in a bottle in the lake. You must retrieve the message while abiding by the following constraints:

   • No one can go in the water to retrieve it.

   • You can only use the tools you have in your possession.

2. A cylinder buried in the ground nearby also contains pertinent information. You must obtain this information while abiding by the following constraints:

   • You cannot lift the cylinder out of the ground.

   • You have to retrieve the message through the hole in the top of the cylinder.

3. When your team has answered all of the "key questions," on the two sheets, see the facilitator for the next clue.

   You have 45 minutes to locate the cylinder and the bottle, retrieve the messages, answer the key questions, and discover the hiding place of the key word.

HUNT FOR THE KEY WORD INFORMATION

1. The poem is talking about *tomorrow*.

2. Sam Slug was looking at a picture of his son. The puzzle "this man's father is my father's son" is easily solved if the word "me" is substituted for "my father's son." The statement then reads, "Brothers and sisters I have none, but this man's father is me."

3. Mount Everest.

4. The nail would be at the same height since trees grow at their tops.

5. The elevator.

HUNT FOR THE KEY WORD INFORMATION

1. The letters should be arranged as follows: o n e w o r d.

2. Neon changed his tire and traveled the last 200 kilometers with four good tires and one flat in the trunk.

3. Too wise you are,

    too wise you be,

    I see you are,

    too wise for me.

4. High powered electrical lines have such a strong magnetic field that it is virtually impossible for birds to land on them. The magnetic field will actually repel the birds.

5. You could not. Mercury is so dense that steel floats in it.

HUNT FOR THE KEY WORD KEY QUESTIONS

1. How would you rearrange the letters in the words "new door" to make one word? (*Note:* There is only one correct answer.)

2. Neon Slick was in a 500-kilometer road rally when he blew one of his tires with 200 kilometers to go. Neon still managed to win the race, even though he went 200 kilometers with a flat tire. None of the other drivers experienced any problems, so how could Neon win with a flat tire?

3. Please translate the following: Y Y U R Y Y U B I C U R Y Y 4 M E

4. Shady was introducing his invention at a "Birds Unlimited" convention. He explained that he developed a special insulation for high-power electrical lines. This insulation is guaranteed to save thousands of birds who unwittingly land on the lines and are electrocuted each year. Shady claimed that with all the birds saved, the annual summer mosquito problem would practically disappear. As Shady was appealing for investors, Captain Frank, an avid bird lover, stood up and told Shady to peddle his line elsewhere. What was wrong with Shady's claim?

5. Suppose you have an open-topped box that is 5 cm × 5 cm × 5 cm (capacity: 125 cubic centimeters). Inside the box is a steel ball bearing that is 25 cubic centimeters in size. Next to the box is a 2-liter pail filled with mercury. How many cubic centimeters of mercury would you have to pour into the box to completely submerge the ball bearing?

When you have the correct answers, please see the facilitator for another clue.

HUNT FOR THE KEY WORD KEY QUESTIONS

1. *Often talked of, never seen,*
   ever coming, never been,
   daily looked for, never here,
   still approaching, coming near.
   Thousands for its visit wait
   but alas for their fate,
   tho' they expect me to appear,
   they will never find me here.

   What is the poem about?

2. Sam Slug was standing in the post office looking at a "wanted" poster. Someone asked him who the man in the poster was and Sam replied, "Brothers and sisters I have none, but this man's father is my father's son." Whose picture was on the poster?

3. Before Mt. Everest was discovered, what was the highest mountain on earth?

4. When Sandy Beach was 6 years old, she hammered a nail into her favorite tree to mark her height. Ten years later, at sweet 16, Sandy returned to see how much higher the nail was. If the tree grew by 5 centimeters each year, how much higher would the nail be?

5. A survey was conducted of all the various mechanical modes of transportation people use to go to work each day. What did it find to be the most common method of transportation?

When you have the correct answers, please see the facilitator for another clue.

KEY WORD

Teamwork

Teamwork is the interactive, continuous process of a group of people learning, working, and growing interdependently to achieve specific goals and objectives in support of a common mission. The interactive, continuous process must be learned.

If you found this key word by working together, CONGRATULATIONS! You're on the right track!

Teamwork is the secret to success. Learning when to compete and when to work together is the challenge.

#18 WHICH HOLE SHOULD I WORK ON?

OVERVIEW

Each team has a PVC tube that contains a ping-pong ball. Each PVC tube has holes in it. Each team must develop a plan to fill its tube with water and float the ball to the top.

OBJECTIVES

- To provide a challenging task that requires creativity
- To have groups utilize creative thinking
- To have team members interrelate and cooperate to achieve team success

GROUP SIZE

Any number of participants divided into teams of three or four members each

MATERIALS

- One 1½-inch diameter PVC tube approximately 7 feet long, capped (sealed) on one end, with holes drilled into it (see Figure 18.1) per team
- One ping-pong ball per tube
- A water supply for each team
- A method for timing the initiative

PHYSICAL SET-UP

Outside, as there is a fair amount of water spillage involved

SUGGESTED TIME

60 minutes (30-minute activity with a 30-minute debriefing)

PROCEDURE

1. Before conducting the initiative, prepare enough PVC tubes for all the groups, using the following directions:

   - Prepare the tubes so they stand high enough that someone cannot pour water directly into the tube while standing on the ground. (They must stand on something.)
   - The holes should be difficult (but not impossible) to seal using fingers, with a set of holes for each team member.
   - There should be enough holes for three to four team members to work simultaneously.
   - Place a ping-pong ball inside each tube.

2. Have the participants separate into teams of three or four members each.

3. Instruct the teams that their task is to retrieve the ping-pong ball from the bottom of the tube using the water supply provided. Answer any questions they may have.

4. Tell participants to begin.

5. After 30 minutes, or when all teams have retrieved their balls, end the activity.

6. Conduct a debriefing session using the following questions:

   - What problems did your team experience?
   - What behaviors helped your team solve the problem?
   - How would you rate your teamwork on a scale of 1 to 10?
   - How did this activity relate to your work environment?
   - How can you use what you have learned back on the job?

QUOTE

"If it is to be, it's up to me."

Unknown

Figure 18.1. Configuration for PVC Pipes

#19 PAPER BAG

OVERVIEW

Using only the materials provided, participants must design a structure that will support at least three reams of paper (about 15 pounds)

OBJECTIVES

- To simulate the value of customer expectations
- To demonstrate the importance of meeting customer expectations
- To learn to use creative thinking when solving problems
- To initiate cooperation between team members

GROUP SIZE

Any number of teams of twelve to twenty people each

MATERIALS

- Twenty paper bags (heavy grocery sacks) per team
- One pair of scissors per team
- One roll of masking tape per team
- Three reams of paper per team
- A method for timing the initiative
- A copy of Handout 19.1 for each team
- A copy of Handout 19.2 for the facilitator

PHYSICAL SET-UP

Indoor room with ample space for the participants to spread out

SUGGESTED TIME

80 to 100 minutes (40-minute activity with a 40-minute to 60-minute debriefing)

PROCEDURE

1. Separate the participants into teams of twelve to twenty participants each.

2. Distribute a copy of Handout 19.1 to each team and ask participants to read it. Respond to any requests for clarification.

3. Advise the teams that there is no secret to this initiative, but that the task does require them to be creative.

4. Instruct the participants to begin.

5. Tell participants when there are 15 and 5 minutes left, and when time has expired.

6. Conduct a debriefing using the following questions:

   • Rate your teamwork on a scale from 1 to 10 and explain the reasoning behind your rating.

   • What did each person contribute to the solution of the problem?

   • What team members' behaviors did you observe that made the team more effective?

   • Would you change anything if you could do it over again? Why? Why not?

   • What have you learned from this experience?

   • In what ways does this experience parallel your current work environment?

   • What insights can you take back to your day-to-day job environment?

QUOTE

"Attitude is the speaker of our present; it is the prophet of our future."

John Maxwell

PAPER BAG TEAM TASK

Your team's task is to design and build a structure within 40 minutes, from the materials supplied, that will support at least three reams of paper (approximately 15 pounds). The structure must stand at least three bags high.

Bonus points will be awarded for design and production efficiency demonstrated by the following points:

- First to complete the task
- Least number of bags used
- Structure that is able to hold the most weight

PAPER BAG SOLUTION

1. Take four bags and place them as shown in Figure 1 below, overlapping them by approximately 3 inches. Tape the bags securely front and back. Note that if only three bags are used, the structure will not meet the "at least three bags high" criteria because of overlapping.

2. Roll the taped bags into a long, tightly rolled tube. Tape the tube securely. Make a total of three of these long tubes.

3. Take one bag and roll it in the direction indicated by the arrow in Figure 2 into a short, tightly rolled tube. Tape the tube securely. You will need a total of three of these tubes.

4. Assemble the six tubes as shown in Figure 3, taping each intersection securely.

> *NOTE:* This is only one of many possible solutions. There are countless others.

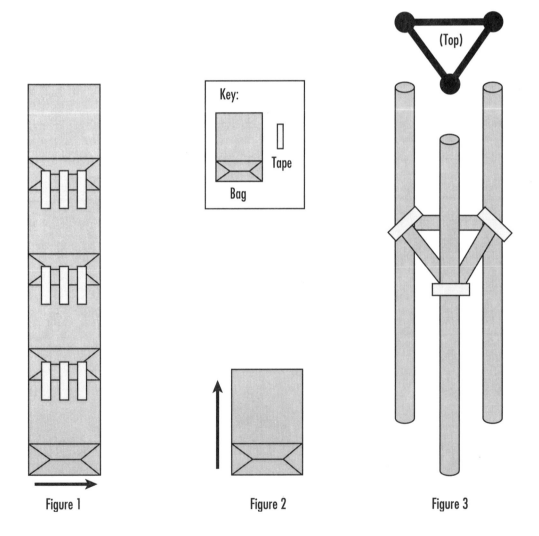

Figure 1   Figure 2   Figure 3

#20 STATE-OF-THE-ART DELIVERY SYSTEM

OVERVIEW

Participants are placed in a nonthreatening environment and challenged to accomplish a task within a limited time. The focus is on production, design, presentation skills, and teamwork with real constraints.

OBJECTIVES

- To experience the dynamics of a team working on a project with time constraints and design requirements and that requires presentation skills

GROUP SIZE

Two to eight teams of four to six participants each

MATERIALS

- At least three eggs per team (have extras!)
- Plastic drop cloths (All drops should occur over drop cloths, for obvious reasons)
- Two 100-count boxes of plastic straws
- One roll of masking tape per team
- Copy of Handouts 20.1, 20.2, and 20.3 for each team
- An envelope for each team
- Rulers (one per team, for measuring the tape used)
- An 8-foot ladder (or other method of obtaining the drop height)
- One copy of Figure 20.1 for the facilitator
- One member of each team must have a method for timing the initiative

PHYSICAL SET-UP

Indoors or outdoors in a space large enough to accommodate all teams without interference. Each team should have a table to work on. If you are conducting this activity indoors, you will need to select a room that has a high enough ceiling to accommodate someone standing on an 8-foot ladder.

SUGGESTED TIME

75 to 85 minutes (30-minute design phase, 20-minute production phase, 5-minute demonstration phase, and a 20-minute to 30-minute debriefing)

PROCEDURE

1. Prior to the activity, put one copy each of Handouts 20.1, 20.2, and 20.3 in an envelope. Prepare as many envelopes as you will have teams.

2. When the group convenes, divide the participants into teams of from four to six each.

3. Give each team an envelope and instruct them to move to a table.

4. Tell the teams to open their envelopes and review the handouts. Make sure all instructions are understood.

5. Tell the teams that once the activity begins you will act as the customer backing the venture and will no longer answer questions. Clarify the expectations of what you want as the customer.

6. Instruct the teams that they will have a maximum of 30 minutes to design the delivery system, 20 minutes to build the system, and 5 minutes to give their presentations and demonstrations. Tell teams that if they finish planning in under 30 minutes they can move on to the production phase.

7. Emphasize the importance of the presentation. Explain that even if their system does not work, an effective presentation may still create the winning device.

8. Explain that during the planning phase each team will be able to request materials with which to build its device. Each team will track its own expenses using Handout 20.2. Explain that you will take requests for materials and distribute them to the teams.

9. Instruct the teams to begin. Inform the teams when there are 10 minutes remaining in the planning phase. Make sure all teams have requested their supplies before the 30 minutes have elapsed.

10. Tell the teams when it is time to move on to the production phase. Inform the teams when there are 5 minutes left and when it is time to stop.

11. Allow each team 5 minutes to present and demonstrate its delivery system.

> NOTE: Make sure spotters are always present when anyone is on the ladder.

12. You will act as the customer awarding the contract. Evaluate each presentation based on the criteria in Handout 20.1 and select the "winner."

13. If no team managed the drop without breaking their egg, see Figure 20.1 for a possible solution.

14. The goal (winning the contract) is important to motivate participants during the activity. However, teams can feel that they have failed if they do not win. Be sure to highlight the positive aspects of the event for all teams (that is, creativity, teamwork, problem solving).

15. Conduct a debriefing session using the following questions:

    • Was your team successful? Why? Why not?

    • What problems did you experience as a team?

    • How would you rate your teamwork on a scale of 1 to 10 (10 being high)? Explain your answer.

    • What strengths did you bring to the team?

    • What contributions from others did you appreciate?

    • Did all members participate? Did any dominate? Explain your answer.

    • Did the team members support one another?

    • Was there a leader who organized the team?

    • What would you change about the activity and why?

    • What have you learned from this experience?

    • In what ways does this experience parallel your current work environment?

    • What insights can you take back to your day-to-day job environment?

QUOTE

"The ultimate responsibility of a leader is to facilitate other people's development as well as his own."

Fred Pryor

STATE-OF-THE-ART DELIVERY SYSTEM INSTRUCTIONS

You are a member of a project team designing a state-of-the-art delivery system for dropping an egg 8 feet onto a hard surface without the egg breaking. There are several corporations vying for this $30-million contract, to be awarded based on the specific guidelines below. Your company needs this contract to stay in business, and many jobs depend on your efforts.

The contract will be awarded according to the following guidelines:

1. You must construct a fail-safe delivery system that meets the 8-foot requirement.

2. You must use the least amount of materials possible in your construction.

3. Only designated materials may be used.

4. You must complete the task as quickly as possible.

5. The maximum time allowed for demonstration is 5 minutes.

6. A spokesperson must make a presentation to the head of the science department of a major university and to businessmen backing the venture. The presentation should include:

   • Name of your delivery system

   • Virtues (distinctive features) of your product

   • Why your design should be chosen above the others

   • A demonstration of how your system works

(All drops are to be performed over a plastic drop cloth.)

> *NOTE:* Breaking the egg may not necessarily eliminate your company from competition. If the other companies have the same problem, the contract will be awarded based on how well the facts were presented.

STATE-OF-THE-ART DELIVERY SYSTEM MATERIALS REQUEST FORM

Materials Use Form

Team Name: _____

Product Name: _____

	Straws (20/pack) $100 pack	Tape (30-inch max) $200/inch	Eggs (3 max) $5000 each
Original request			
Additional			
Actual			
Cost (each)			
Total cost (actual x cost)			

STATE-OF-THE-ART DELIVERY SYSTEM TIME TRACKING SHEET

Appoint one member of your team to be the timekeeper. The timekeeper should monitor and record the amount of time the team uses for each phase.

Time Tracking

	Planning	Production	Presentation
Allowed	30	20	5
Used			

Figure 20.1. Possible Solution

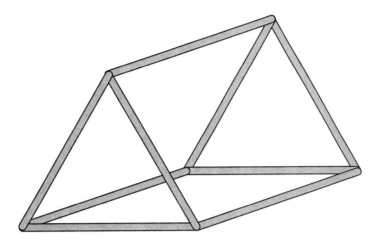

The frame layout (pictured above) is made of straws taped together. The egg, wrapped in tape, is suspended inside this frame using more tape. This is by no means the only possible solution, but it has been successful on many occasions.

#21 SPACE ANTENNA

OVERVIEW

Each group represents a company that is competing with other companies for a research and development contract for a space antenna. Each group has to design and construct a space antenna that will earn as much money as possible.

OBJECTIVES

- To allow participants to experience the development of a project proposal
- To demonstrate the fundamentals of creating team results via team structure
- To learn how a facilitator works within a team project

GROUP SIZE

At least two teams of four to eight members each, with no limit on the number of teams

MATERIALS

- One copy each of Handouts 21.1, 21.3, 21.4, 21.5, and 21.6 for each team
- A copy of Handout 21.2 for each team facilitator
- Lego's® building blocks or the equivalent for construction of an antenna
- A flip chart
- A felt-tipped marker
- A measuring tape
- A method for timing the initiative

PHYSICAL SET-UP

Indoors or outdoors in a space large enough so that each team can work at a table without disturbing any other teams

SUGGESTED TIME

90 to 120 minutes (45 minutes for the proposal, 15 minutes for construction, and a 30-minute to 60-minute debriefing)

PROCEDURE

1. Begin by reviewing the objectives of the activity with the participants.

2. Form participants into teams of four to eight members.

3. Seat each team at a different table.

4. Explain to the teams that you will serve as the customer; then distribute copies of Handouts 21.1, 21.3, 21.4, 21.5, and 21.6 to each team.

5. Instruct the teams to read Handout 21.1 to learn what the task is and what is expected of them. Clarify any questions they might have.

6. Once each team has identified a facilitator, distribute a copy of Handout 21.2 to each team facilitator and instruct them to read the handout.

7. Tell the teams that the team facilitators will have control of the materials for each team and that they will "purchase" what is required.

8. Tell the teams that they have 45 minutes to design their antenna and practice for the construction phase. Remind them they have to submit a project proposal (Handout 21.6) to you at the end of this time.

9. Take notes and observe the behaviors of each team during the design phase. Assure that the teams are following the constraints in their handouts.

10. After the 45 minutes are over, request that each team turn in its project proposal and disassemble its antenna in preparation for the construction phase.

11. Start the construction phase and allow the teams 15 minutes. Call out the elapsed time to each team as it indicates that it has completed construction and post the time on the flip chart.

12. Remind the teams that their structures must stay standing for 30 minutes.

> NOTE: Tell the teams that the structure must stand as long as possible if this is an all-day workshop and this is the opening initiative.

13. Observe and take notes for the debriefing session.

14. At the end of the construction phase, record the time, number of pieces used, and height of the antenna for each team on the flip chart.

15. Ask each team to fill in the "actual" and "profit" columns on Handout 21.4 and to tally their final scores.

16. Determine which team achieved the most profit.

17. Conduct a debriefing session using the following questions:

- How would you rate your teamwork on a scale of 1 to 10, with 10 being the highest?
- What positive contributions did your team facilitator make?
- Do you now have a clearer understanding of the role of a facilitator?
- What behaviors did you appreciate from your team members? From the team facilitator?
- What behaviors made you successful?
- Would you do anything differently if you could do the activity again?
- What did you learn? (Go around the group and ask each participant to review his or her personal insight.)
- How can you relate this to a team you have been on in your work environment?
- In what ways does this activity parallel your current work environment?
- What insights can you take back to your day-to-day job environment?

QUOTE

"As a manager, the important thing is not what happens when you are there but what happens when you are not there."

Ken Blanchard and Robert Lorber

SPACE ANTENNA INSTRUCTIONS FOR TEAMS

1. Preparation Phase

   - Organize your group in any way that seems most effective.

   - Select a team member to serve as facilitator.

   - Use Handout 21.3 to decide on profit targets for the following:

     —Cost

     —Height

     —Time

   - Record your profit goals on Handout 21.4.

2. Project Design Phase (45 minutes)

   - You are allowed to handle and assemble materials during the design phase, but pieces must be disassembled before beginning the construction phase in order to give all companies an equal start at construction time.

   - You must develop detailed plans for actual construction, as your profit will be linked to how quickly you can assemble your space antenna during the construction phase.

   - Read Handout 21.5 for an explanation of how to complete the project proposal (Handout 21.6) and then complete your team's proposal.

   - Once completed, submit your proposal to the session facilitator (the customer).

3. Construction Phase (15 minutes)

   - The session facilitator will signal the beginning of the construction phase. All teams will start at the same time.

   - Your team should signal the session facilitator immediately when it has completed construction so that an accurate time can be recorded.

   - At the completion of your construction, note the number of pieces used and the height of the structure.

   - The structure must remain standing without any additional support at the end of the construction phase and for at least 30 minutes after that.

SPACE ANTENNA TEAM FACILITATOR'S INSTRUCTIONS

1. In your role as team facilitator, you will guide your team through this project using your understanding of the following:

   • The ultimate result of this project will be to win the contract by pleasing the customer and spending the least on the best space antenna.

   • This project was undertaken because the demand for space antennas is projected to increase to $100 billion by the year 2010.

   • This project is important to your company's business objectives because some of the company's current products are becoming obsolete.

   • If the company does not win this contract, it may go out of business.

2. Be sure the relationship between you and the team members is agreed on.

3. Be sure members of the team have identified and understand their roles and responsibilities.

SPACE ANTENNA PROJECT EFFECTIVENESS SHEET

Cost Effectiveness

Number of Pieces	Profit
10	+ $100,000
15	+ $50,000
20	+ $35,000
25	+ $25,000
30	+ $10,000
35	− $5,000
40	− $30,000
45	− $150,000

Height Effectiveness

Height in Inches	Profit
70	+ $150,000
65	+ $120,000
60	+ $70,000
55	+ $20,000
50	0
45	− $150,000
40	− $300,000

A bonus of $15,000 per inch above 70 inches will be added.

Time Effectiveness

Seconds	Profit
30	+ $200,000
60	+ $150,000
90	+ $100,000
120	+ $50,000
150	+ $15,000
180	0
210	− $30,000
240	− $80,000

For every 5 seconds your group takes beyond the time projected for completion, it will be penalized $10,000.

For every 5 seconds you are ahead of the time projected for completion, the team will be awarded $5,000.

SPACE ANTENNA TEAM PROFIT TARGETS

	Target	Actual	Profit
Cost Effectiveness (# of pieces)	————	————	————
Height Effectiveness (height in inches)	————	————	————
Time Effectiveness (time in seconds)	————	————	————

Total Profit ————

SPACE ANTENNA INSTRUCTIONS FOR COMPLETING A PROJECT PROPOSAL

The Project Proposal Form in Handout 21.6 serves two purposes. First, it is a vehicle for communicating your team's focus to the customer and gives him or her information for choosing among different teams' proposals. Second, it assists the team itself in reaching clarity on the end result, the benefits, the roadblocks, and the effects on the rest of the organization. Use the project proposal to formally define your team's goal for winning the space antenna contract.

The project proposal includes:

- *A statement of the goal.* A statement developed by the team that describes the end result of the project.

- *Desired and possible benefits or outcomes.* Brainstorm all possible benefits or results (both measurable and general) from the project. This will give the team a sense of the potential value of the project and also produce a list of measures for a project's success. It shows why the team selected its particular goal.

- *Critical concerns or roadblocks.* Brainstorm all possible concerns team members have or roadblocks to the success of the project. Identify key people who must buy into the project and decide ways to anticipate and handle resistance. You will then know the obstacles and challenges you face to winning the contract.

- *Affected parties.* Brainstorm all individuals, teams, departments, and others who may be affected by the work or product of the group. Of course, the entire company will be affected if the team loses the contract.

- *Support required.* If there is any additional support necessary (a change in the time frame or additional team members or expertise needed), this is the opportunity to request it. During this activity, you may request all the support you need.

SPACE ANTENNA PROJECT PROPOSAL

Team: _____ Date: _____

Team Members:
(* indicates team leader)

_____

_____

_____

1. Goal statement

_____

_____

_____

_____

2. Desired or possible benefits (measurable and general):

3. Critical concerns or potential roadblocks:

4. Departments or other projects affected:

5. Support required (equipment, expertise, money, people)

#22 MOUNTAIN LION AND RABBIT

OVERVIEW

Participants are asked to solve a problem for a farmer who owns a rabbit, a mountain lion, and some carrots. Following given constraints, the farmer must take the two animals and the carrots across a river within 15 minutes without any losses.

OBJECTIVES

- To encourage lateral thinking
- To demonstrate that sometimes we have to take a step backward in order to progress forward
- To demonstrate that problem solving is easier in groups

GROUP SIZE

Any size group

MATERIALS

- One copy of Handout 22.1 for each participant
- One copy of Handout 22.2 for the facilitator
- A method for timing the initiative

PHYSICAL SET-UP

Inside in a classroom setting

SUGGESTED TIME

45 to 50 minutes (15-minute to 20-minute activity with a 30-minute debriefing)

PROCEDURE

1. Distribute one copy of Handout 22.1 to each participant and instruct them to read it.

2. Make sure that all participants understand the task, then tell them that they have 15 minutes to complete the task, and tell them to begin.

3. (Optional) If participants are unsuccessful at solving this problem individually, allow them to form into teams and try to solve it collectively. Allow 5 minutes.

4. Use Handout 22.2 to explain the solution to everyone.

5. Conduct a debriefing session using the following questions:

   - What made this problem difficult to solve?

   - What was the key behavior you used to solve the problem?

   - What can we learn from this experience?

   - In what ways does this experience parallel your current work environment?

   - What insights can you take back to your day-to-day job environment?

   - (Optional) If you worked within a team, did it make solving the problem easier? Why?

QUOTE

"Fires can't be made with dead embers, nor can enthusiasm be stirred by spiritless men. Enthusiasm in our daily work lightens efforts and turns even labor into pleasant tasks."

James Mark Baldwin

MOUNTAIN LION AND RABBIT SITUATION

Problem: A farmer has a rabbit, a mountain lion, and some carrots. He wants to take the animals and the carrots across a river in the next 15 minutes.

Constraints:

- Only one item at a time can be carried across the river. If the mountain lion is left with the rabbit, he will eat it. If the rabbit is left with the carrots, he will eat them.

- No cages, muzzles, ropes, or other restraints are available.

- The facilitator must approve your plan.

How would you help the farmer cross the river safely?

MOUNTAIN LION AND RABBIT SOLUTION

If participants cannot figure out the solution, share the following with them.

1. Take the rabbit across the river and leave it.
2. Go back to the other side.
3. Take the carrots across the river and leave them.
4. Go back to the other side, taking the rabbit with you.
5. Leave the rabbit and cross the river again with the mountain lion.
6. Go back across again.
7. Take the rabbit across the river with you; you are finished!

#23 THE SWAMP

OVERVIEW

Groups must move from a safe area, over a "swamp" (a 40- to 45-foot barrier of noxious substances) to the other side. The goal is to have the entire group accomplish the task, not just the most capable members.

OBJECTIVES

- To allow group members to work together to achieve a goal
- To work toward a goal safely and without incident
- To incorporate differing levels of individual adeptness to reach a common goal

GROUP SIZE

Eight to forty participants

MATERIALS

- Four 6-foot lengths of PVC pipe, approximately 12 inches in diameter
- One 8-foot long pole that is very sturdy
- One 50-foot rope
- Two 4-foot lengths of rope
- One 2-inch × 12-inch board, 10 feet long
- A copy of Figure 23.1 for the facilitator

PHYSICAL SET-UP

A large indoor or outdoor space that allows movement for all group members.

> *NOTE:* Do not set up this initiative on a smooth surface. The PVC pipes will move too quickly and someone will fall. A wrestling mat, gymnasium floor exercise mat, or heavily carpeted area is recommended when using this initiative indoors.

SUGGESTED TIME

60 to 90 minutes (30-minute to 40-minute activity with a 30-minute to 50-minute debriefing)

PROCEDURE

> *SAFETY NOTE:* This activity involves bending, stretching, and kneeling. Have all participants do some stretching to warm up prior to the activity. Spotting the participants as they cross the "swamp" on the board is a necessity. Be sure to maintain everyone's safety at all times.

1. Prior to this activity, set up the "swamp" using the 4-foot pieces of rope to delineate the area.

2. When ready to begin, explain to the participants that their task is to get everyone across the "swamp" safely.

3. Provide them with the following materials:
   - Four 6-foot long PVC pipes
   - One 8-foot long pole
   - One 50-foot length of rope
   - One 2-inch × 12-inch board, 10 feet long

4. Explain the following to the participants:
   - The two 4-foot ropes delineate the area to be crossed, which is filled with viscous primordial ooze.
   - The swamp substance extends indefinitely in a lateral direction past the measured area. It is impossible to walk around this swamp.
   - If a participant touches the swamp, even slightly (remember, this stuff is devastating!), he or she must return to the starting point.
   - The board and the rope will dissolve if any part of them touches the swamp. If this happens, the group will need to re-form at the starting point and will have to start the initiative over, but this time no talking will be allowed.
   - The PVC tubes and the 8-foot long pole are swamp-resistant and come in contact with this viscous primordial ooze.

- Walking into the swamp in order to advance the group's efforts is not allowed and is obviously unhealthy.
- Facilitators, because of their specially imported swamp-resistant shoes, may move freely within the confines of whatever nasty substances their imaginations placed there.

5. After all participants have safely crossed the swamp, conduct a debriefing session using the following questions:
   - What was your initial reaction to this task?
   - What was required to solve this problem?
   - How effectively did the group collaborate on solving the problem?
   - In what ways does this activity parallel your current work environment?
   - What insights can you take back to your day-to-day job environment?

QUOTE

"Burnout is when you lose sight of where you want to go."

Unknown

Figure 23.1. Solution to The Swamp

Place the PVC pipes and the board as shown below. Have the first two participants to cross the swamp step on the board, with one participant holding one end of the rope and the other the 8-foot pole. Have someone who remains on the starting side of the swamp hold the other end of the rope. Each participant must use the 8-foot pole to push across, like a boat on a real swamp. As the board rolls forward, the tubes at the rear must be placed at the front. Repeat until the swamp has been crossed. At this point, one of the participants who crossed returns, pulling on the rope, and picks up another participant. This continues until everyone has crossed. The last two participants are pulled across with the rope.

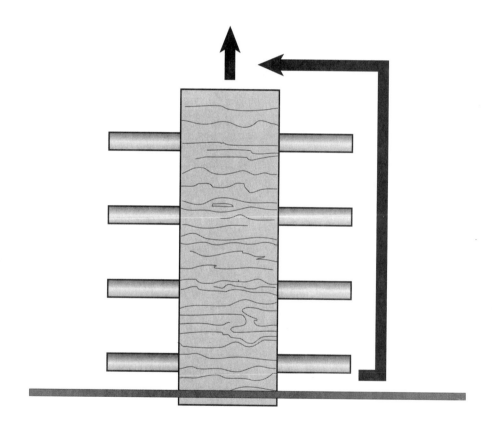

#24 HIGH TIDE ISLANDS AND JAWS*

OVERVIEW

Team members stand on an "island" for 15 seconds in the first round. Beginning with the second round, the island begins to shrink until it is only a small portion of its original size. Participants are told that sharks will devour anyone who falls off the island. The team must decide how to solve the problem.

OBJECTIVES

- To develop communication skills
- To increase team initiative by allowing teams to develop methods of solving problems together in simulated crises
- To develop better listening skills as a result of processing information between team members

GROUP SIZE

Six to twelve participants

MATERIALS

- Four fabric squares or wooden platforms in the following sizes:
  52 inches × 60 inches
  39 inches × 45 inches
  26 inches × 30 inches
  13 inches × 15 inches
- A method for timing the initiative

PHYSICAL SET-UP

A large open indoor or outdoor area that allows for movement of all participants

---

*This activity was created by Harry Johnson, Palm Bay, Florida.

SUGGESTED TIME

60 minutes (30-minute activity with a 30-minute debriefing)

PROCEDURE

> *SAFETY NOTE:* Some movements during the activity may require facilitator spotting.

1. Tell the participants that their task is to keep everyone on an "island." Explain that the water around the island is infested with sharks and that participants can only step off the island when you give the "all clear" signal.

2. Place the 52-inch × 60-inch "island" on the floor and instruct all participants to stand on it together.

3. After 15 seconds, give the "all clear" signal and tell the team to step off the island.

4. Explain that the tide is coming in rapidly and replace the 52-inch × 60-inch "island" with the 39-inch × 45-inch "island" and repeat Steps 2 and 3.

5. Repeat the process using the 26-inch × 30-inch square and then the 13-inch × 15-inch square.

6. After the four rounds are complete, debrief using the following questions:

   - What was your initial reaction to being together on the "island"?
   - What was required in order to solve this problem?
   - How effectively did the group collaborate on solving the problem?
   - In what ways does this activity parallel your current work environment?
   - What insights can you take back to your day-to-day job environment?

QUOTE

"Athletic competition doesn't develop character, it exposes it."

Unknown

#25 DOES YOUR MIND ALWAYS WORK?*

OVERVIEW

Participants demonstrate that even simple movements can be difficult under certain circumstances.

OBJECTIVES

- To demonstrate how the brain responds to visual and verbal messages
- To demonstrate that physical manipulation can confuse messages to the brain

GROUP SIZE

Any number of participants

MATERIALS

None

PHYSICAL SET-UP

Indoors or outdoors (a classroom setting works best)

SUGGESTED TIME

20 minutes (5-minute activity with 15-minute debriefing)

PROCEDURE

1. Ask for a volunteer to stand in front of the group.
2. Ask the volunteer to stand with his or her arms extended in front of the body, wrists crossed, and fingers locked. (Demonstrate if necessary)

---

*This activity was adapted from an original concept given to me by Peter Crumley, Melbourne, Florida.

3. Ask the volunteer to bring his or her locked hands up and underneath so that the hands are near—but not touching—their chest.

4. Tell the volunteer that you will now point to a finger and to *immediately* try to raise that finger. Emphasize "immediately." (If given enough time to think, the volunteer likely will be able to do it.) Also, be sure not to touch the finger you want raised.

5. Make sure the volunteer has understood the instructions. Point to one of the volunteer's fingers and observe as he or she tries to raise it. It will be extremely hard for the volunteer to move the finger you point at.

6. Have the remaining participants form dyads.

7. Instruct the pairs to try what they have just witnessed. Have them alternate roles so both can try it.

8. Explain that the message is that the mind controls certain aspects of our bodies, and even simple things can be difficult under the right conditions.

9. Conduct a debriefing session using the following questions:

   • Why does this phenomenon occur?

   • What does this tell us about our visual senses and learning predictability?

   • Can we be tricked by directions?

   • In what ways does this experience resemble your current work environment?

   • What insights can you take back to your day-to-day job environment?

QUOTE

"It's a mistake to think we listen only with our ears. It's much more important to listen with the mind, the eyes, the body, and the heart. Unless you truly want to understand the other person, you'll never be able to listen."

Mark Herndon

#26 THE PROBLEM

OVERVIEW

Participants use two buckets to measure out exactly 4 gallons of water required to fill STS-666's "transplastoclapometer" pod so that a launch, the only opportunity for the next 138 years, can proceed.

OBJECTIVES

- To utilize creative thinking skills
- To complete a task successfully under time restrictions

GROUP SIZE

Two to four per team with no limit on number of teams

MATERIALS

- One empty 5-gallon bucket per team
- One empty 3-gallon bucket per team
- A copy of Handout 26.1 for each team
- Water supply (if the wet option is chosen)
- Handout 26.2 for the facilitator
- A method for timing the initiative

PHYSICAL SET-UP

If you conduct this activity outdoors, let the teams actually use water. If you are indoors, then you may wish to just simulate the filling of the buckets with water (focusing on the actions required to obtain the required 4 gallons of water).

SUGGESTED TIME

25 to 30 minutes (10-minute to 15-minute activity with 15-minute debriefing)

PROCEDURE

1. Divide the participants into teams of two to four members each.

2. Give each team one 3-gallon and one 5-gallon bucket.

3. Distribute a copy of Handout 26.1 to each team. Have the participants read the handout and then ask if there are any questions.

4. If the "wet" option is to be used, show the teams where the water supply is located.

5. Tell the participants they will have 10 minutes to solve the problem and instruct them to begin.

6. Observe their processes and take notes.

7. After the 10 minutes have elapsed or all teams have solved the problem, call an end to the activity. Reveal the solution if no one was able to solve the problem.

8. Conduct the debriefing session using the following questions:

   • Why was this a difficult problem to solve?

   • What contributed to your success or failure?

   • Did the time constraint affect your ability to solve the problem?

   • Did working with teammates help or hinder the problem-solving process? In what way?

   • In what ways does this activity parallel your current work environment?

   • What insights can you take back to your day-to-day job environment?

QUOTE

"From the clash of differing opinions comes the spark of truth."
Unknown

THE PROBLEM TASK SHEET FOR TEAMS

Space Shuttle "Redundant" sits on launch pad 34C awaiting takeoff. Its mission, designated STS-666, is to photograph the newly discovered planet Tralfamador. There are only 10 minutes left of the last day of a 4-day launch window. Launch attempts the previous 3 days were canceled. The next opportunity for this important mission will not come for another 138 years due to Tralfamador's peculiar orbit. THE SHUTTLE MUST BE LAUNCHED TODAY!!

Unfortunately, it seems that one of the shuttle technicians just "forgot" the 4-gallon bucket of water needed to fill the transplastoclapometer pod. Unless the team can figure out a way to measure out the required 4 gallons of water within the remaining 10 minutes before launch using only the 3-gallon and 5-gallon buckets available, the mission will have to be scrubbed.

Your team must measure out 4 gallons of water for the transplastoclapometer within 10 minutes.

THE PROBLEM SOLUTION SHEET

1. Fill the 3-gallon bucket.

2. Dump it into the 5-gallon bucket.

3. Fill the 3-gallon bucket again and use it to completely fill the 5-gallon bucket, *leaving 1 gallon of water in the 3-gallon bucket.*

4. Empty the 5-gallon bucket completely, and pour the 1 gallon from the 3-gallon bucket into it.

5. Fill the 3-gallon bucket with water.

You will have 1 gallon of water in the 5-gallon bucket and 3 gallons in the 3-gallon bucket, a total of 4 gallons.

#27 I'LL KNOW IT WHEN I SEE IT*

OVERVIEW

Teams must determine the decision-making process that an organization is using when choosing to accept or reject a card.

OBJECTIVES

- To understand the value of obtaining information in various forms
- To see the importance of cooperation with others
- To learn how to use different approaches to solving problems
- To provide a simple method for teams to examine their problem-solving styles

GROUP SIZE

Two people to a team, with a maximum of six teams

MATERIALS

- A deck of regular playing cards
- A copy of Handout 27.1 for each team or an overhead transparency or flip-chart sheet made from Handout 27.1

PHYSICAL SET-UP

A large table with enough chairs around it for all participants. It is important that each participant be able to see each card as it is played.

SUGGESTED TIME

60 to 75 minutes (30-minute to 45-minute activity with a 30-minute debriefing)

---

*This activity was adapted from an original concept by Dick Teach at Georgia Tech.

PROCEDURE

1. Separate the group into teams of two. Designate Team A, B, C, and so on, until all teams have been named.

2. Either distribute a copy of Handout 27.1 to each team or display the information on an overhead transparency or flip chart.

3. Review the process and task if necessary so that all participants understand.

4. Deal out as many cards from the deck as you can, giving each team an equal number, *retaining at least one card.* See the chart below.

   Two teams = 25 cards each; dealer = 2;

   Three teams = 17 cards each; dealer = 1;

   Four teams = 12 cards each; dealer = 4;

   Five teams = 10 cards each; dealer = 2;

   Six teams = 8 cards each; dealer = 4.

5. Tell the teams that their task will be to determine how you (the dealer) are making the decision about whether to accept or reject each card as a team plays it. Allow the teams to discuss the problem with one another if they choose to do so, but do not make an issue of them doing so.

6. Explain that the teams will play their cards in order, with Team A going first, followed by Team B, then Team C, and so on.

7. You will then make the decision to accept or reject each card as it is played according to the following criteria, which are *not to be revealed to participants:*

   • After a black card, accept only even-numbered cards

   • After a red card, accept only odd-numbered cards

   • Jacks, Kings, and Aces are *even*; Queens are *odd*

   > NOTE: Study these criteria until you understand them completely. They are hard to remember even when you know the key.

8. Lay down one card and ask Team A to play its first card. Accept or reject it according to the criteria described in Step 7. Then ask Team B to play its card, then Team C, and so forth, as you accept or reject each.

9. Periodically, ask the teams how they are making their decisions about which cards to play.

10. Continue playing until your decision-making method is discovered or until the teams have played all of their cards.

11. If all of the cards are played without anyone discovering your method, then reveal it to the group.

12. Conduct a debriefing session using the following questions:

- What difficulties did your team experience?

- Did your team share information with other teams?

- Did you use standard card-handling methods such as keeping them so that only you could see them? Did anyone say to do this? Did you need to do it?

- How did you interpret the instructions? Did they help you during the process? In what way?

- What changes in your thinking process could you have made in order to improve the outcome of this experience?

- In what ways does this experience parallel your current work environment?

- What insights can you take back to your day-to-day job environment?

QUOTE

"A moment's insight is sometimes worth a lifetime of experience."

Ernest Holmes

I'LL KNOW IT WHEN I SEE IT TEAM TASK

Each team, in order, plays its cards (the input) to complete the task. The dealer (the organization) makes the decision to accept or reject your input.

Your task is to determine what decision-making process your organization (the dealer) is using when choosing to accept or reject your input (a card).

#28 DID YOU SAY "AIRCRAFT"?

OVERVIEW

Each team independently designs and builds an "aircraft" using only the materials provided and selects a "pilot" to give a demonstration to a "customer." The customer awards a "contract" based on the distance and accuracy of the aircraft's demonstration flight.

OBJECTIVES

- To demonstrate that breakthrough thinking is often essential
- To stimulate thinking "out of the box"
- To understand the boundaries in a given situation
- To avoid imposing arbitrary or unimportant restrictions
- To demonstrate teamwork through group decision making

GROUP SIZE

Six to twelve participants per team

MATERIALS

- Two large rubber bands for each team
- One small golf pencil with approximately 12 inches of masking tape rolled around it for each team
- One large sheet of flip-chart paper for each team
- A copy of Handout 28.1 for each team
- Items for marking the boundaries
- A method of measuring distance
- A method for timing the initiative

PHYSICAL SET-UP

This activity requires an open area in which participants can demonstrate their proto-types. Set up some boundaries to measure distance and accuracy. For example, if you are conducting this activity outdoors, the goal could be to propel the aircraft as far as possible while remaining within the boundaries formed by trees, stakes, rope, or what-ever. Indoors, chairs or rope could be used to mark the boundaries. An example is illus-trated below:

Figure 28.1. Suggested Placement of Boundaries

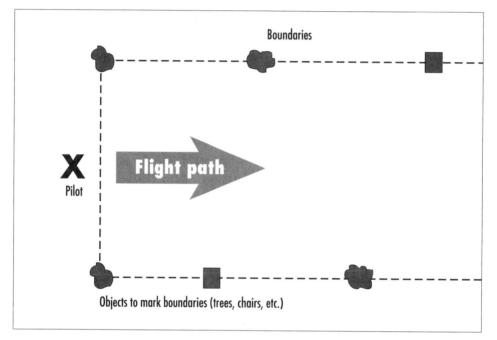

SUGGESTED TIME

50 minutes (15 minutes for completion, 5 minutes for the competition, and 30-minute debriefing)

PROCEDURE

1. Divide the group into teams of six to twelve members each.

2. Give each team a copy of Handout 28.1, two rubber bands, a small golf pencil with 12 inches of masking tape rolled around it, and a large sheet of flip-chart paper.

3. Direct the teams to read the handout, and answer any questions they might have.

4. Instruct the teams that the goal is to design and build an aircraft that will win the competition, and thus the contract, within the constraints identified in Handout 28.1.

5. Remind each team that this is a competition for length and accuracy of flight.

6. Tell the teams to begin the task.

7. Let them know when there are 5 minutes remaining and when time has elapsed.

8. Bring the teams together and ask each team's "pilot" to demonstrate the accuracy and distance of the team's aircraft.

9. Measure each team's "flight" and award the contract to the team whose aircraft went the farthest while remaining within the designated boundaries.

> *NOTE:* The key here is that what is asked for is an "aircraft," not necessarily an "airplane." The most effective aircraft design I have seen used consists of wadding the sheet of paper up into a ball, wrapping it with the tape and rubber bands, and throwing it like a baseball.

10. Conduct a debriefing session using the following questions:
    - Did your team think within certain boundaries?
    - What does this tell us about our thinking process?
    - What can we learn from this activity?
    - In what ways does this experience parallel your current work environment?
    - What insights can you take back to your day-to-day job environment?

QUOTE

"You always pass failure on your way to success."

Unknown

DID YOU SAY "AIRCRAFT"? TASK FOR TEAMS

Your company's future depends on winning the contract for a new aircraft design. Can you win the special competition for your company?

You have 15 minutes to independently design and build an aircraft that meets customer requirements using the materials provided.

Customer criteria on which the contract will be awarded are as follows:

- Distance of flight
- Accuracy of flight

Demonstrations to the customer will start in 15 minutes.
The following constraints apply:

- You can use only one prototype and one test pilot.
- You may use only the materials provided!
- There is a 15-minute time limit.

#29 MAKING THE NEWS*

OVERVIEW

Teams compete to supply the news to a major television network.

OBJECTIVES

- To demonstrate the importance of intra-team communications for successfully completing a task
- To experience the process of creating and managing ideas under pressure
- To identify skills required for a task and then to utilize them appropriately

GROUP SIZE

Teams of ten to sixteen participants each, split as equally as possible into three sub-teams: editorial, journalism, and production

MATERIALS

- Copies of all of the day's newspapers for each team
- A television set in each room with an all-news channel playing
- Pens, paper, flip-chart paper, colored pens, and paints for each team
- One video camera with VCR, monitor, and playback facilities
- A supply of videotapes
- One copy of Handout 29.1 for each team
- Extra video camcorders for roving reports
- A method for timing the initiative

PHYSICAL SET-UP

Each team requires its own room, which must be divided into three work areas. A separate room is used by all teams for filming the news.

---

*This activity was created by Roger Woodgate, director of ABA Consultants Ltd, 59 High Street, Royston Herts SG8 9AW, United Kingdom.

SUGGESTED TIME

205 minutes (10-minute briefing, 120-minute activity, and a 75-minute debriefing)

PROCEDURE

1. Distribute copies of Handout 29.1 to the teams and review it with them.

2. Explain to the teams that the activity is competitive and the "contract" will go to the team that best meets the criteria as laid out below:

   - Delivers two 5-minute news items on time
   - News items have a lead-in that will grab the attention of the viewer
   - Provides variety in reporting
   - Stays within budget
   - Uses varied visual stimuli

3. Explain that each team must split into three groupings—editorial, journalism, and production—that will have separate work areas. Say that the groups will be monitored in terms of degree to which they stick to their roles as described in Handout 29.1.

4. Explain that during the planning phase the following constraints must be observed:

   - Teams must book studio time with the facilitator on a first-come, first-served basis. Studio time is limited to two 10-minute slots and teams must keep to the time allotted. Studio time costs $100.00 per minute. Remind teams of the budget considerations noted in Handout 29.1.
   - Filming must be completed within 30 minutes from the time the decision is made to start filming.
   - Two editorial meetings must be held during the planning phase.

5. Lead each team to its work room and instruct each team to begin.

6. During the planning phase, circulate from room to room, noting any incidents that might be used during the debriefing. Also, keep track of studio time used and money spent by each team. Periodically let the teams know how much time remains.

7. At the end of the production phase, bring all the teams together to view all the news items and announce the winner.

8. Debrief the activity using the following format:

- Ask each team to work in its subgroups (editorial, journalists, production) and to review the following:

  Their own performance

  How they would improve their own communication if they had a chance

  How they worked with the other two groups

- Bring the three subgroups together to share comments on the following:

  Key learning(s)

  Comments on intra-team performance

  How creativity was managed

  How competition was managed

- Finally, ask each group to summarize its findings for the entire group

QUOTE

"The news never changes, it just happens to different people."

Unknown

"MAKING THE NEWS" BRIEFING FOR PARTICIPANTS

Your company has tendered an offer for a contract to provide a regular prime-time news bulletin for a national television network. As part of the selection process you have been asked to produce two 5-minute sample news programs on tape. The tape must be completed by the cut-off time.

First assign departmental roles within your team as follows:

- *Journalism Team:* Responsible for generating news items, creating stories, and presenting material to Editorial Team.

- *Editorial Team:* Responsible for the compilation of news items and final decisions on content.

- *Production Team:* Responsible for producing the news tape and managing the technical requirements.

The team's task is to produce two 5-minute news broadcasts of today's news on video. The content is up to you to decide as a group, but should reflect an agreed-on editorial balance between topics, for example:

Lead stories	Financial
Home	Features
Foreign	Crime
Fashion	Sport

Your budget is $2,000. The following charges apply:

- You will be charged for studio time booked and not utilized.

- Video cameras can be hired at a cost of $150 per 5 minutes for "roving" reports.

- The following penalties will apply:

  Failure to hold editorial meeting = $500

  Every minute late when due in studio = $200

  Late production of 5-minute video = $750

  Failure to complete full 5-minute video =$1,000

The following constraints apply:

- You must book studio time with the facilitator in advance. Studio time is limited to two 10-minute slots, and you must use the time that was allotted.

- Studio time costs $100 per minute. The facilitator will take into consideration teams that have underspent their budgets.

- Filming must be completed within 30 minutes from the time the decision is made to start filming.

- Two editorial meetings must be held during the planning phase.

- You have 120 minutes to plan and produce your videos.

#30 BLIND PUZZLE*

OVERVIEW

This is a powerful activity that can be used to test and strengthen a team's problem-solving skills. The group is taught a simple problem-solving model, then practices the model.

OBJECTIVES

- To teach and practice effective group problem-solving skills
- To demonstrate a team's communication and organizational skills

GROUP SIZE

Any number of teams of eight to thirteen participants each. The optimum team size is one participant for each piece of the puzzle.

PHYSICAL SET-UP

Indoors or outdoors, with a table or flat work area for each team

SUGGESTED TIME

30 to 75 minutes (15-minute to 30-minute activity with 15-minute to 45-minute debriefing)

MATERIALS

- One blindfold for each participant
- One giant jigsaw puzzle (twelve to fifteen pieces) or equivalent for each team.+

---

*This activity is from Jeff Boyd of Operation Explore, North Palm Beach, Florida.

+A puzzle with the Operation Explore Group Problem-Solving Model (the model presented here) on it is highly recommended (available through Operation Explore, Inc.).

- A flat surface for each team, preferably a table large enough so that the entire team can help to put the puzzle together
- A method for timing the initiative

PROCEDURE

1. Tell the group that their goal is to learn and practice a very simple yet extremely powerful problem-solving model.

2. Ask the group to memorize it:
   - Identify the problem(s)
   - Identify the resources
   - Brainstorm
   - Plan
   - Implement the plan
   - Evaluate

3. Once you have presented this to the group, ask them to repeat it by asking them "What is Step A . . . Step B . . . Step C?" and so on.

4. Once they have learned the Group Problem-Solving Model, tell the participants that they are now ready to move on to the next challenge.

5. Separate the group into teams of eight to thirteen members each (the optimum number of members for the team corresponds with the number of pieces in the puzzle).

6. Direct the teams to select a table, and have them gather around it.

> NOTE: Do *not* have the puzzles on the tables where the teams can see them!

7. Inform the teams that you are going to give them a problem (state it as a "problem" and not a "puzzle" to force the group to identify the problem as a jigsaw puzzle) to solve, but that, as in real life—where most problems blindside us—in order to make this as realistic as possible, everyone will have to put on a blindfold. Give each participant a blindfold and have them put them on.

8. When all team members are blindfolded, tell them the following:
   - Each of you will be given a piece of the problem.
   - You must maintain physical contact with your piece of the problem until it becomes a part of the solution.
   - You must keep your blindfolds on until you agree as a team that you have successfully solved the problem.
   - Please do not begin until I say so.

> *NOTE:* If there are leftover pieces to the puzzle (that is, there are fewer participants than puzzle pieces), inform the team(s) that "These additional problems will be left with you" (or you can just quietly leave the additional pieces of the puzzle on the table without them knowing).

9. Verify that everyone understands the task, give one puzzle piece to each team member (and, if applicable, place the remaining pieces of the puzzle on the team's table), and have that team begin. Repeat with additional teams as necessary.

10. When all team puzzles are finished (or time has expired), tell the participants that they may remove their blindfolds.

11. After the puzzle is put together, ask participants to review the problem-solving model they learned earlier and to decide which step they used first. (Nearly every group will have started with Implement the Plan.) Explain that they were each trying to solve their own pieces of the puzzle and not their group's puzzle.

12. Conduct a debriefing using the following questions:

    - How did you do as a team?
    - Did you use the group problem-solving method presented at the beginning of this session?
    - What step did you start with? What step should you have started with?
    - What are the ramifications for this type of problem solving?
    - Do you ever feel like this at work? In what way?
    - What do the blindfolds represent?
    - What are some metaphors or analogies that you can draw from this activity?

QUOTE

"A nod is as good as a wink to a blind man."

Unknown

#31 WING IT*

OVERVIEW

Each participant is given a wing nut to put on a threaded rod. Participants compete to see which team can take all its wing nuts across the rod in the shortest amount of time.

OBJECTIVES

- To give participants a task to work on together
- To learn to use cooperation and teamwork to win
- To process individual input to influence group problem solving
- To show that continuous improvement is advantageous in any work environment

GROUP SIZE

Five to thirty participants grouped into teams of five or six each

MATERIALS

- One 12-inch long threaded rod per team
- One wing nut that fits the threaded rod per participant
- A copy of Handout 31.1 for each team
- A method for timing the initiative

PHYSICAL SET-UP

Inside in a location that has round tables

SUGGESTED TIME

35 minutes (10 minutes to practice, 5 minutes to complete, and a 20-minute debriefing)

---

*This activity was adapted from an original concept by Jim Cain of Eastman Kodak.

PROCEDURE

1. Separate the participants into teams.

2. Distribute one threaded rod per team and one wing nut per participant.

3. Give one copy of Handout 31.1 to each team and instruct team members to read it.

4. Tell everyone that you are the customer and will answer any questions they have.

5. Tell the teams that they have 10 minutes to practice, and that they should begin practicing right away.

> NOTE: Sometimes 10 minutes is too much time. If you feel the teams are ready to move on, just say, "Time is up."

6. Ask for a team to volunteer to go first and time the team as it completes the task.

7. Time each team as it completes the task.

8. Award the "contract" to the team with the shortest time.

9. Conduct a debriefing session using the following questions:

   • What issues did your team face?

   • How did your team overcome them?

   • What behaviors did your team members exhibit that were effective?

   • What elements of teamwork did you experience during this activity?

   • What role did continuous improvement play?

   • In what ways does this activity parallel your current work environment?

   • What insights can you take back to your day-to-day job environment?

QUOTE

"Frustration is not having anyone to blame but yourself."
Unknown

WING IT TEAM INSTRUCTIONS

Your objective: To win the contract

Measure of success: The contract will be awarded based on speed. The team that can complete the task in the shortest amount of time will win the contract.

Requirements: Each person's wing nut must be placed on the same end of the threaded rod and traversed across the length of the rod.

Timing: You will have 10 minutes to practice before the "customer" (the facilitator) times your attempt.

#32 WORKPLACE FOR EMPOWERMENT

OVERVIEW

Participants are asked to design an ultimate working environment.

OBJECTIVES

- To lead into a discussion on changes in the workplace
- To have participants discuss choices they make about their ideal workplaces
- To demonstrate the similarities that exist among individuals
- To identify issues in the current work environment in a safe, nonthreatening, and fun way

GROUP SIZE

Any size group

MATERIALS

- Paper for participants
- A flip chart
- Pens or pencils for participants
- Felt-tipped markers
- A method for timing the initiative

PHYSICAL SET-UP

Indoors with chairs and tables or other writing surfaces for participants

SUGGESTED TIME

60 minutes (20-minute design session, 20-minute sharing session, and a 20-minute debriefing)

PROCEDURE

1. Separate the group into teams of four or more, or if the group is small have them perform the task individually.

2. Inform the teams that they have been asked by the CEO to design a work environment for a new factory being built next year. They should include all aspects of the environment, from working conditions to investment in research and development.

3. Tell the teams that they have 20 minutes to design an ideal work environment before sharing their designs with the total group.

4. After 20 minutes, have the teams share their ideas.

5. As an option after the initial task, ask participants to use all of their ideas together to design an ideal work environment.

6. Conduct a debriefing session using the following questions:

   • Why did you select this type of work environment? Address any issues you thought were important.

   • Are there any similarities between what people wanted in their ideal environments?

   • Do you think that people generally wanted the same things?

   • How does your design differ from your current work environment?

   • Do any of the new designs resemble your current work environment?

QUOTE

"The quality of employees will be directly proportional to the quality of life you maintain for them."

Charles Bryan

#33 WORLD'S BEST PRODUCT

OVERVIEW

A team must design and build a product from the supplied materials and sell it to the group on the basis of two 5-minute presentations—one on the virtue and the other on the value of the product.

OBJECTIVES

- To experience working together in a nonthreatening environment
- To use creativity and innovation to develop and sell a product
- To incorporate participants' strengths and weaknesses into a production task
- To develop sales techniques and use them to sway a group
- To develop presentation skills

GROUP SIZE

Five to ten per team, with at least two teams, although four are recommended

MATERIALS

- 1 K'Nex® set,* Tinker Toys®, or equivalent building set per team
- A method for timing the initiative

PHYSICAL SET-UP

Indoors or outdoors
SUGGESTED TIME
120 minutes (60-minute activity, with a 60-minute debriefing)

---

*Call 1-800-KID-KNEX for sales information.

PROCEDURE

1. Separate the participants into teams of from five to ten members each.

2. Give each team a prepackaged building toy set.

3. Tell the teams that they are to design and build a product from the materials supplied and then prepare two 5-minute presentations, one on the *value* and one on the *virtue* of the product they develop.

4. Tell the teams that they have 60 minutes to develop their products and prepare their presentations.

5. After 60 minutes, ask each team to give its presentations.

6. (Optional) Give rewards for the best product or rank them in order according to appeal, use, or time taken to build.

7. Conduct a debriefing session using the following questions:

   - What behaviors helped your team to be successful?

   - Was it difficult designing a product that you had no research knowledge for?

   - Can you relate this to any difficulty your company has had in designing new products?

   - What can be learned from this experience about designing new products?

   - What can you learn from this activity about teamwork?

   - In what ways does this activity parallel your current work environment?

   - What insights can you take back to your day-to-day job environment?

QUOTE

"Additional problems are the offspring of poor solutions."

Mark Twain

#34 PUZZEL*

OVERVIEW

This activity, although simple and easy to use, sends a powerful message. The participants are challenged to solve a puzzle and must listen to and synthesize the specific input from all of the group members to be successful. To be truly effective, teams must develop communication systems. The dynamics in this initiative are powerful for all aspects of team building or information processing within a group, as well as for creative problem solving.

OBJECTIVES

- To demonstrate shared accountability
- To demonstrate personal accountability and creativity
- To discover effective communication techniques for use within (and between) teams
- To illustrate the importance of effective planning and clear understanding
- To illustrate the dynamics of processing team members' information
- To give participants the opportunity to break away from old paradigms and self-imposed limitations

GROUP SIZE

Between seven and twelve participants

MATERIALS

- A copy of Handout 34.1 for the facilitator
- A copy of Handout 34.2 for the facilitator
- One copy each of Handouts 34.3, 34.4, 34.5, and 34.6, cut in strips
- A copy of Handout 34.7 for each participant

---

*This initiative was created by Brian Jackson, president of The Orion Trust.

167

- A method for marking 30-inch ¥ 30-inch squares (rope, masking tape, flip-chart paper, cloth, or chalk)
- A method for timing the initiative

PHYSICAL SET-UP

Ideally, the activity area is selected to create the illusion of a long, narrow space (along a wall, confined on the other side by tables, hedges, or whatever). A narrow walkway works well too.

SUGGESTED TIME

60 to 75 minutes (30-minute activity with a 30-minute to 45-minute debriefing)

PROCEDURE

1. Prior to the activity, review Handouts 34.1 and 34.2.

2. Prepare Handouts 34.3, 34.4, 34.5, and 34.6 by copying each page and cutting it apart on the dotted lines. Do not label the handouts. Each of the four handouts contains four unique individual handouts that seem identical but contain different information needed by the participants.

3. Prepare the squares ahead of time as shown on Handout 34.3. Eight participants are assumed for the example in the handout, but more or less can be used. If there is an odd number of participants, for example, five on one side and four on the other, you would need to set up a total of eleven spaces, leaving one of the spaces at one end empty, in addition to the middle empty square.

4. If more than one team will be participating, have them spread out far enough apart so as to minimize any contact between them, whether verbal or visual.

   > NOTE: If you intend that there be the possibility of collaboration between the teams, then keep them within sight of one another.

5. Lead the team(s) to the activity area, stand in the middle square yourself, and ask the participants to stand in the others (if there are an odd number of participants, have them leave one of the squares on the end empty). Tell everyone to face you (the two groups will now be on either side of the center square, facing one another).

6. Inform the participants that these are their "initial designated positions." Step out of your square so that all team members can see you, and tell them that you are going to give each of them some information, and they must read it thoroughly before proceeding.

7. Distribute the sixteen paper strips you have cut out from Handouts 34.3, 34.4, 34.5, and 34.6 to the team members, with any extra handouts (depending on the total number of participants) going to people at the ends, rather than those in the middle.

8. Tell the participants to read their handouts and begin the activity.

9. After the 30 minutes are up, end the activity and share the solution if the team was not able to come up with it on its own.

10. Conduct a debriefing session by either distributing copies of Handout 34.7 and asking teams to discuss the answers among themselves or by using the following questions:

- Was all available information shared and understood in a timely manner before the group jumped into action?

- Did all team members have a clear vision of what they were supposed to do?

- Was there brainstorming and a synthesis of key information?

- Were roles and responsibilities defined?

- How long did the team members stay in their boxes before realizing that they were at liberty to problem solve and plan in a more conducive location or configuration?

- What was the team's problem-solving strategy? Explain.

- How well did the team members listen to and support one another?

- How was frustration handled within the team? Explain.

- How was leadership handled? Explain.

- Was there an effort to solicit contributions from all team members, or did someone take charge and tell them what to do? Which method was more successful?

- Was there a strategy to experiment with, to test and re-test solutions? What was the strategy? How successful was it?

- Was a strategy developed to deal with the silent aspect of the demonstration to the facilitator? What was that strategy? Did the team experiment with and test the solution?

- What false assumptions or artificial constraints did team members place on themselves? Why?

- If more than one team worked on the puzzle, what was the relationship between them?

- (If applicable) In what ways could team members have been more proactive in sharing ideas, thereby developing a win-win strategy?

- In what ways does this experience parallel your current work environment?

- What insights can you take back to your day-to-day job environment?

PUZZEL FACILITATOR INFORMATION

Each of the sixteen individual paper strips you cut out contain the following generic information:

> *"Starting from your initial designated positions, you are required to reposition your-selves in a particular configuration. The information on your strip of paper may only be shared with others verbally. Each of you has additional information related to this activity."*

The following pieces of information appear on only one of the sixteen strips:

- "You have 30 minutes to complete the project."
- "You must reposition yourselves so that those of you standing on the right side of the center space end up on the left side of the center space."
- "You will have *only one* opportunity to demonstrate your solution to the facilitator."
- "The center space must be empty at the conclusion of your repositioning."
- "You must reposition yourselves so that those of you starting on the left side of the center space end up on the right side of the center space."
- "Everyone must remain facing in his or her original direction during the execution of all moves."
- "You may move into an empty space only if it is immediately in front of you."
- "No one may move backward."
- "Only one person may move at a time."
- "In order to be successful, you must adhere to all project constraints."
- "You may move around a person *only* if that person is immediately in front of you, is facing you, *and* there is an empty space directly behind that person."
- "There are only two legitimate moves."
- "Only one person can be in a space at a time."
- "The demonstration of your team's solution for the facilitator must be done in *total silence.*"
- "You must notify the facilitator when your team is prepared to demonstrate its solution."
- "The configuration of the spaces on the ground may not be modified in any way."

PUZZEL SOLUTION SHEET

The solution to this puzzle is deceptively simple. Often, one team member will identify the principle behind the solution, but will have a hard time convincing other team members. At any one time, there are always two possible moves. One move will create a logjam, wherein two people going the same direction move next to one another. The necessary process is to move in a "staggered" way, with participants from each side leaving a blank space or a person from the other side between them.

Sample solution for an eight-person team:

To begin with, participants are on positions 1, 2, 3, and 4, facing right. Position 5, the center, is empty. The remaining four participants are on positions 6, 7, 8, and 9, facing left.

The following moves lead to a successful solution:

4 to 5; 6 to 4; 7 to 6; 5 to 7; 3 to 5; 2 to 3; 4 to 2; 6 to 4; 8 to 6; 9 to 8; 7 to 9; 5 to 7; 3 to 5; 1 to 3; 2 to 1; 4 to 2; 6 to 4; 8 to 6; 7 to 8; 5 to 7; 3 to 5; 4 to 3; 6 to 4; 5 to 6

This leaves the eight participants in the correct ending positions, as shown below:

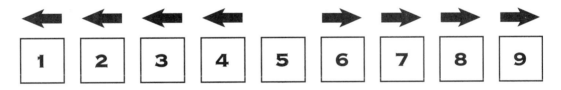

PUZZEL

Starting from your initial designated positions, you are required to reposition your-selves in a particular configuration. Each of you has additional information related to this activity, specifically that you have 30 minutes to complete the project. The informa-tion on this sheet may only be shared verbally.

PUZZEL

Starting from your initial designated positions, you are required to reposition your-selves in a particular configuration. Each of you has additional information related to this activity, specifically that everyone must remain facing in his or her original direc-tion during the execution of all moves. The information on this sheet may only be shared verbally.

PUZZEL

Starting from your initial designated positions, you are required to reposition your-selves in a particular configuration. Each of you has additional information related to this activity, specifically that you may move into an empty space only if it is immedi-ately in front of you. The information on this sheet may only be shared verbally.

PUZZEL

Starting from your initial designated positions, you are required to reposition your-selves in a particular configuration. Each of you has additional information related to this activity, specifically that only one person may move at a time. The information on this sheet may only be shared verbally.

PUZZEL

Starting from your initial designated positions, you are required to reposition your-selves in a particular configuration. Each of you has additional information related to this activity, specifically that in order to be successful you must adhere to all project constraints. The information on this sheet may only be shared verbally.

PUZZEL

Starting from your initial designated positions, you are required to reposition your-selves in a particular configuration. Each of you has additional information related to this activity, specifically that you must reposition yourselves so that those of you stand-ing on the right side of the center space end up on the left side of the center space. The information on this sheet may only be shared verbally.

PUZZEL

Starting from your initial designated positions, you are required to reposition your-selves in a particular configuration. Each of you has additional information related to this activity, specifically that you will have *only one* opportunity to demonstrate your solution to the facilitator. The information on this sheet may only be shared verbally.

PUZZEL

Starting from your initial designated positions, you are required to reposition your-selves in a particular configuration. Each of you has additional information related to this activity, specifically that the center space must be empty at the end of your reposi-tioning. The information on this sheet may only be shared verbally.

PUZZEL

Starting from your initial designated positions, you are required to reposition your-selves in a particular configuration. Each of you has additional information related to this activity, specifically that those of you starting on the left side of the center space must end up on the right side of the center space. The information on this sheet may only be shared verbally.

PUZZEL

Starting from your initial designated positions, you are required to reposition your-selves in a particular configuration. Each of you has additional information related to this activity, specifically that no one may move backward. The information on this sheet may only be shared verbally.

PUZZEL

Starting from your initial designated positions, you are required to reposition your-selves in a particular configuration. Each of you has additional information related to this activity, specifically that you may move around a person *only* if that person is immediately in front of you, is facing you, *and* there is an empty space directly behind that person. The information on this sheet may only be shared verbally.

PUZZEL

Starting from your initial designated positions, you are required to reposition your-selves in a particular configuration. Each of you has additional information related to this activity, specifically that there are only two legitimate moves. The information on this sheet may only be shared verbally.

PUZZEL

Starting from your initial designated positions, you are required to reposition your-
selves in a particular configuration. Each of you has additional information related to
this activity, specifically that only one person can be in a space at a time. The information on this sheet may only be shared verbally.

PUZZEL

Starting from your initial designated positions, you are required to reposition your-
selves in a particular configuration. Each of you has additional information related to
this activity, specifically that the demonstration of your team's solution for the facilitator must be done in *total silence.* The information on this sheet may only be shared verbally.

PUZZEL

Starting from your initial designated positions, you are required to reposition your-
selves in a particular configuration. Each of you has additional information related to
this activity, specifically that you must notify the facilitator when your team is prepared
to demonstrate its solution. The information on this sheet may only be shared verbally.

PUZZEL

Starting from your initial designated positions, you are required to reposition your-
selves in a particular configuration. Each of you has additional information related to
this activity, specifically that the configuration of the spaces on the ground may not be
modified in any way. The information on this sheet may only be shared verbally.

PUZZEL SELF-MANAGED REVIEW SESSION

Spend about 20 minutes discussing your overall performance as a team. Look back over the time the team spent on this project and answer the following questions:

1. In what ways did we work effectively together, and why (both within your own team and, if applicable, with other teams)?

2. In what ways could we have more successfully completed this project? Why?

3. What are some helpful insights, parallels, and/or reminders that we can take from this activity back to our working environment?

To help you manage your discussion time effectively, consider the following questions:

1. Was everyone informed and clear about our mission? How effective were we in identifying a good strategy and appropriate roles and responsibilities before tackling the project?

2. How well did we listen to everyone, organize ourselves, and plan to maximize our resources?

3. How clear were we about our operating constraints, and how well did we seek information from one another?

4. How pleased are we with the way we developed ideas together, and did we utilize a wide variety of individual talents and strategies to solve the problem?

5. How flexible and creative were we when faced with difficulty in finding a quick solution or in dealing with any inter-team or intra-team conflict?

6. If applicable, what false assumptions did we make or artificial constraints did we place on ourselves? Why did we do this?

7. How much did a preoccupation with "turf" issues hamper a rapid and effective solution?

8. (If applicable) In what ways are we pleased about the nature and quality of our relationship(s) with the other teams?

9. (If applicable) Were teams basically competing against one another, or were we trying to work collaboratively?

10. How would we rate our levels of trust and effective communication within (and, if applicable, between) our team(s)?

11. (If applicable) In what ways could we have been more proactive in sharing ideas and solutions among teams?

12. Can we identify parallel situations in our work environment?

#35 DR. ROSE VS. DR. BUCKLEY

OVERVIEW

Dr. Rose and Dr. Buckley work on solutions for curing disease and ending world hunger, respectively. The key to solving both problems is an ingredient in Pyro, produced by NASA and grown only once a year during scheduled space missions. In order for both doctors to solve their problems, an agreement has to be reached between them and NASA, and they must determine a win-win solution for themselves.

OBJECTIVES

- To allow participants to experience conflict in a different context from what they are used to
- To require participants to use conflict-management skills
- To establish group needs
- To compare needs with other teams to see if they are in conflict and at what level
- To find ways to solve seemingly unsolvable problems

GROUP SIZE

Eight to twelve participants, in pairs

MATERIALS

- Enough copies of Handout 35.1 for each participant in the Dr. Buckley role
- Enough copies of Handout 35.2 for each participant in the Dr. Rose role
- A method for timing the initiative

PHYSICAL SET-UP

Indoors

SUGGESTED TIME

30 to 40 minutes (10-minute to 20-minute activity with a 20-minute debriefing)

PROCEDURE

1. Tell the participants to separate into teams of two.

2. Have the two members of each dyad decide which role they want to play:
   - Dr. Buckley, research scientist working on a secret project for the government, or
   - Dr. Rose, research scientist for a medical research firm

3. Have the dyads spread out to separate areas (separate rooms or different areas of the same room).

4. Give each person a copy of his or her respective handout and instruct everyone to read only the handout received.

5. Remind the participants of the 20-minute time limit, then have them begin their role-play discussions.

6. Observe the interaction in each dyad and take notes for debriefing.

> NOTE: The best resolution is for Dr. Rose to get the juice and Dr. Buckley to get the skin. If participants look for a win-win solution and share their needs openly, it will allow them to make the best decision.

7. Keep track of the dyads that decide on the win-win method and have them go last during the debriefing. This allows the others to see how they missed the simple concept of win-win.

8. Conduct a debriefing session using the following questions, starting with teams that had the most difficulty resolving the conflict and continuing to the teams that had the least difficulty:
   - (Ask each team in turn) How did you eventually resolve the conflict?
   - What did you learn from this experience?
   - In what ways does this experience parallel your current work environment?
   - What insights can you take back to your day-to-day job environment?

QUOTE

"A diamond is a chunk of coal that made good under pressure."

Unknown

ROLE-PLAY SHEET FOR DR. BUCKLEY

You are a research scientist whose company is working on a secret project for the government. In your work you have created a substance you call "Nutride." Your group discovered by accident that Nutride, when sprayed on vegetables, causes the food to grow at five times the normal rate. This only seems to affect vegetables. In addition, once Nutride is sprayed on the vegetables, the plants no longer need watering. This product could ultimately eliminate world hunger! Your team knows that all the ingredients needed to make Nutride are very common, with the exception of Pyro skin.

Unfortunately, the only place Pyro has been successfully cultivated and grown is on-board space stations in a weightless atmosphere. NASA has given your group a small sample for research purposes.

The African continent has been going through its worst drought in nearly 100 years. It has lasted over 6 months, with no relief in sight. Record high temperatures have emptied most of the water supplies. The crops have dried up and food is scarce. Thousands of people have already died. Relief efforts by other countries have helped, but this alone is not enough. African governments are desperate and crying for help.

Your company has just recently patented Nutride. Your company also knows that if you can obtain all the ingredients needed to produce enough Nutride, it could be sold to those African governments and millions of dollars could be made. Furthermore, millions of lives would be saved, and your company would be credited with ending world hunger.

It would take all the remaining supply of Pyro that NASA has to meet your needs. NASA has no plans to grow more until some time next year. Your company has authorized you to offer NASA up to $5 million for the Pyro skin that it needs.

You have also heard that Dr. Rose, a research scientist for another organization, needs the remaining supply of Pyro as well. Before approaching NASA, you have decided to talk to Dr. Rose in hopes of persuading him not to bid on the Pyro. You are aware that you, personally, stand to make millions of dollars and also become a world renowned scientist if you can help save the African people. It is imperative that you obtain the Pyro. You will have 20 minutes in which to discuss the situation with Dr. Rose.

ROLE PLAY SHEET FOR DR. ROSE

You are a scientist for a major medical research company that has recently developed a vaccine to prevent lositus, a rare but very contagious disease that attacks the brain. Symptoms of this disease include brain swelling, headaches, hallucinations, and great pain. The disease has always proven fatal, but because the disease is extremely rare, your research has not been considered that valuable in the past.

However, there has been an outbreak of lositus in a small town in northern Mexico, just a few miles from the California border. If the community is not quarantined and soon given the lositus vaccine, this disease could rapidly spread to the United States, and, eventually, worldwide.

If the company you work for can produce enough vaccine to save these people and stop a potential world epidemic, it will certainly make a great deal of money, even though the economy is in the midst of a recession. Furthermore, the company will receive worldwide publicity, which means that future business deals will be guaranteed.

Unfortunately, one of the main ingredients used to make the vaccine comes from the juice of Pyro. The only place Pyro has been successfully cultivated and grown is onboard space stations in a weightless environment. NASA had originally given your company a small sample of the Pyro for research purposes. NASA also has just enough Pyro left so that an adequate supply of the vaccine can be produced. NASA has no plans to grow more Pyro until next year.

Realizing the windfall your company would receive by stopping this potential epidemic, you have been authorized to offer NASA $5 million for the remaining Pyro supply.

You have also heard that Dr. Buckley, a research scientist for another organization, needs the Pyro for a project that he is working on. Before approaching NASA, you have decided to talk to Dr. Buckley in hopes of persuading him not to bid on the Pyro. You realize that you personally stand to make millions of dollars and become a world renowned scientist if you can help save this town. You have 20 minutes in which to discuss the situation with Dr. Buckley.

#36 SAVE THE BUCKET

OVERVIEW

Using only the materials supplied, teams must remove a bucket from the center of a circle without physically entering the circle or dragging or dropping the bucket.

OBJECTIVES

- To allow team members to practice their planning skills
- To establish effective communication between team members
- To allow team members to demonstrate innovation

GROUP SIZE

Eight to ten participants per team

MATERIALS

- One 3-gallon empty plastic bucket per team
- One roll of masking tape per team
- One 10-penny nail per team
- One ball of string or twine per team
- One 8-foot long, 2-inch × 2-inch board per team
- Six large rubber bands per team
- 55 feet of rope laid out into a circle with a radius slightly larger than 8 feet
- Handout 36.1 for the facilitator
- A method for timing the initiative

PHYSICAL SET-UP

An open field, lawn, or other level surface outdoors or a large room indoors

SUGGESTED TIME

75 to 90 minutes (45-minute activity with a 30-minute to 45-minute debriefing)

PROCEDURE

1. Prior to the activity, lay out each rope to form a circle. Adjust the circle according to the degree of difficulty you wish to achieve or physical limitations of the group. Place the bucket in the middle of the circle.

2. Tell each team that the goal is to remove the bucket from the circle using only the materials provided.

3. Instruct the teams that they must complete the task while abiding by the following constraints:

   • Team members cannot enter the circle.

   • The bucket cannot be dragged or dropped.

   • Each team has 45 minutes to complete the task.

   > *NOTE:* Add other constraints if appropriate.

4. Tell participants that if they drop or drag a bucket, you will replace the bucket in the center of the circle and the team must start again.

5. Instruct participants to begin.

6. After all teams have completed the task (or when time is over, whichever comes first), conduct a debriefing session using the following questions:

   • How many of you thought this task was impossible?

   • What difficulties did you or your teammates experience?

   • What role did creativity play in your team's outcome?

   • Did your team process all inputs from various team members?

   • What made your team successful? Unsuccessful?

   • What behaviors did you appreciate from other team members?

   • What can you learn from this experience?

   • In what ways does this activity parallel your current work environment?

   • What insights can you take back to your day-to-day environment?

QUOTE

"Knowledge is the only instrument of production that is not subject to diminishing returns."

J. M. Clark

SAVE THE BUCKET SOLUTIONS

Two possible solutions follow:

- Wrap one of the rubber bands around the head of the nail. Tape the nail securely to the end of the board. Select the team member who has the most upper body strength to hold the board in one hand. Have one (or more as necessary) team members take that person's free hand, allowing that person to lean further into the circle and hook the handle of the bucket with the nail and lift it out.

- Tie string or twine to the end of the board, then tie the other end of the string or twine about one fourth of the distance down the nail. Use tape to secure the string to the nail. Wrap the rubber bands tightly around the bottom of the nail (as a counterweight), allowing the nail to be used as a hook. As if it were a fishing pole, use the nail to hook the handle of the bucket and lift the bucket from the circle.

#37 TEAM WALK

OVERVIEW

Each team must move from Point A to Point B and back to Point A again on "skis" by holding onto rope handles.

OBJECTIVES

- To allow participants to experience teamwork on a fundamental level
- To encourage cooperation among participants
- To demonstrate that quick decision making is sometimes necessary
- To demonstrate that sometimes we lead or are led by others

GROUP SIZE

At least two teams of between eight and eleven members each. Additional people can act as spotters or observers.

MATERIALS

- Two pieces of wood 4 inches × 4 inches × 12 feet for each team, assembled according to Figure 37.1
- Twenty-two ¾-inch, 4-foot long ropes for each team, half for each ski
- A stop watch
- A copy of Figure 37.1 for the facilitator
- A method for timing the initiative

PHYSICAL SET-UP

A large, open, flat area either indoors or out

SUGGESTED TIME

60 to 90 minutes (30-minute to 45-minute activity with 30-minute to 45-minute debriefing)

PROCEDURE

1. Prior to the activity, assemble the "skis" according to the instructions in Figure 37.1.

2. Select a beginning point (Point A) and a turnaround point (Point B). They should be at least 40 to 45 feet apart. If possible, designate separate points for each team. Mark each point in some way.

3. Divide the participants into teams of between eight and eleven members each. If anyone has trouble participating for any reason, assign that person to be a coach.

4. Explain the task to the teams: Each team must transport its entire group from Point A to Point B and return to Point A as quickly as possible while standing on "skis."

5. Identify Point A and Point B for the teams.

6. Explain the following rules:

   - Everyone's feet must remain on the boards the entire time.

   - No contact is allowed with the ground. (Decide the penalty for touching the ground, such as starting over, a time penalty, etc.)

   - The turn must be 180 degrees.

7. Review safety issues and make sure everyone is comfortable with participating.

8. Answer any questions, then tell the team(s) to begin. If there is room for more than one course, have teams compete against one another at the same time. If not, time each team's performance with the stop watch.

9. After all teams have finished, conduct a debriefing session using the following questions:

   - How would you rate your teamwork on a scale of 1 to 10? Explain.

   - What behaviors (cooperation, listening, trust, etc.) did you feel contributed to your success as a team?

   - What can we learn about teamwork from this experience?

   - What is one thing you did really well as a team?

   - How did your team adjust when something was not working?

   - Was the workload distributed equally among team members?

   - How committed were you to achieving the team's goal?

   - Did being timed affect your decision-making process?

   - How well did you listen to other team members?

   - How active were you in building other members' self-esteem?

   - What lessons can you take back to your current job environment?

QUOTE

"There's always room for improvement—it's the biggest room in the house."

Louise Heath Leber

Figure 37.1. Ski Assembly

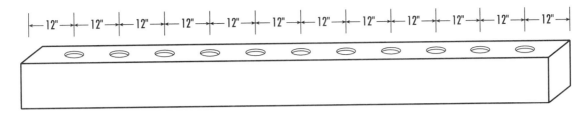

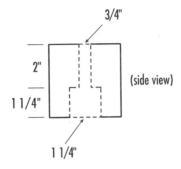

To prepare the boards, drill a ¾-inch wide hole ¾ of an inch deep on top of each board every 12 inches. Then turn the board over and drill 1¼-inch holes 1¼ inches deep at the same places in the board so that the two holes meet.

To assemble the skis, tie a knot in one end of each 4-foot length of rope and feed the rope through the larger holes on the bottom of each ski and out the smaller hole on top. The knot will go up into the "ski" so that the bottom will remain flat.

When you are finished, you will have two skis with eleven ropes coming out the top. Each participant will have one rope on each ski to hold onto. They will have to determine among themselves how to handle extra ropes.

OVERVIEW

Three research teams are located on three separate islands that are surrounded by acid. Each team receives assignments meant for other teams, so teams must transport members to the appropriate islands so that the required tasks can be performed.

OBJECTIVES

- To experience learning during conflict
- To plan and execute a successful strategy
- To utilize team members' input for successfully completing tasks
- To use strategic planning and negotiating skills
- To learn to work successfully when under pressure

GROUP SIZE

Three teams with four to six people per team and two or three people on the management team (optional)

MATERIALS

- Figure 38.1, which shows the layout of the "islands"
- Four 38-foot long pieces of rope for designating the four islands
- A method for cleaning hands after the activity
- A method for timing the initiative

For Alpha Team:

- A copy of Handout 38.2
- Three 2-inch × 8-inch boards, 8 feet long
- Two cement blocks
- One 55-gallon drum
- Two 1-gallon buckets
- Three Zeno (oranges)

- One walkie-talkie*

For Beta Team:
- A copy of Handout 38.3
- Two 2-inch × 8-inch boards, 8 feet long
- One cement block
- Two 55-gallon drums
- Two 1-gallon buckets
- Three Zeno (oranges)
- One walkie-talkie*

For Charlie Team:
- A copy of Handout 38.4
- Two 2-inch × 8-inch boards, 8 feet long
- Two cement blocks
- One 55-gallon drum
- Two 1-gallon buckets
- Three Zeno (oranges)
- One walkie-talkie

For Management Team: (Optional, depending on the number of participants available)
- A copy of Handout 38.1
- A copy of Figure 38.1
- One walkie-talkie

PHYSICAL SET-UP

Outdoor wooded area

SUGGESTED TIME

105 minutes to 170 minutes (60-minute to 110-minute activity with 45-minute to 60-minute debriefing)

PROCEDURE

1. Prior to conducting this activity, locate the proper setting and lay out the "islands" with rope as shown in Figure 38.1.

2. Make copies of the appropriate handouts for the four teams, then place them in envelopes on the team's island, as shown below:
   - Management Team: Handout 38.1 and Figure 38.1
   - Alpha Team: Handout 38.2
   - Beta Team: Handout 38.3
   - Charlie Team: Handout 38.4

---

*Walkie-talkies add some extra fun to the activity, but they are optional. If they are not used, the Management Team must find a way to communicate with other groups.

3. Make sure that you are familiar with all the requirements and constraints from each team's handout. For example, the Zeno fruit can be transferred only on the Island of Hope, but only the management team has that information. Management's viewpoint on the Zeno may be clouded by the promise of dollar awards. This will potentially generate a struggle between management and team members.

4. Place the other materials on each island as specified in the Materials section.

5. After the group convenes, form the teams and send them to their specific islands. The management team will be located away from the four islands. They will communicate with the teams by walkie-talkie (if available) or in writing. If there are not enough participants to use a management team, play the role yourself.

6. Instruct the teams to open their envelopes and read the handouts. Tell everyone that from this point on, you will answer only questions that clarify the task or address safety conditions.

7. Instruct the teams to begin.

> NOTE: The number of Zeno fruit (oranges) needed is a distraction added to generate conflict. If the teams really look at their needs, they will realize that one team needs the skin, another the seeds, and another the juice. Thus, if the teams work together, they can all achieve their goals.

> NOTE: The management air drop can be moved up to 10 minutes if the activity is run without the aid of walkie-talkies. You may also decide that an air drop is not required. The main focus is to create conflict for the teams and management to work out.

8. After the groups finish, conduct a debriefing session using the following questions:

- How did you interpret your team's task?
- What type of problems did your team face?
- How helpful was the management team?
- What do you think helped your team be successful or unsuccessful?
- How would you rate your teamwork on a scale of 1 to 10, with 10 being the highest? Explain.
- How was conflict handled within your team? With other teams?
- Did the teams cooperate with one another? What were the issues?
- Did any team look for the winning outcome?
- How was leadership handled on your team? How effective was it?
- In what ways does this experience parallel your current work environment?
- What insights can you take back to your day-to-day job environment?

QUOTE

"It's not the employer that pays the wages. Employers only handle the money. It's the customer who pays the wages."

Henry Ford

Figure 38.1. Layout for Research Islands

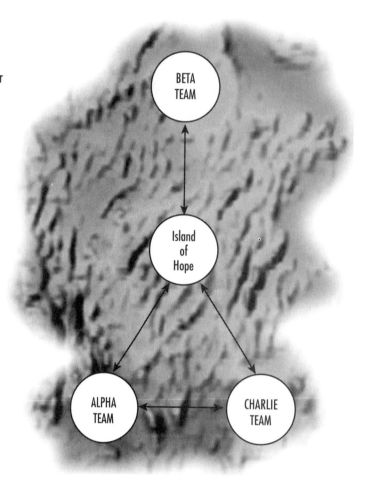

Executive Team is located out of sight of the other teams

BETA TEAM

Island of Hope

ALPHA TEAM

CHARLIE TEAM

RESEARCH TEAM MANAGEMENT TASK

You are members of International University's Executive Management Team responsible for a major research project in a remote area of the world. The teams in the field are the Alpha Team, Beta Team, and Charlie Team. They are on three separate islands surrounded with acid. Their exact locations are shown on Figure 38.1. You have just been informed that the manpower assignments have been mixed up and the individuals with the expertise required to perform the various experiments are not present on the proper islands.

This research project has been publicized as a study of human habitation in remote areas of the world. The real purpose of the experiments is to conduct research of major benefit to all mankind.

1. The Alpha Team experiment is to develop a way to increase the utilization of the human mind by 50 percent.

2. The Beta Team research, if successful, will eliminate most birth defects.

3. The Charlie Team is developing a new vaccine that they hope will eliminate all forms of cancer.

These experiments may represent the most important breakthrough in history, thus it is critical to relocate specialists to the right islands.

There also appears to be a major problem with the rare Zeno fruit being used in the experiments. None of the teams seem to have enough of the fruit to perform their experiments. Your group may have to decide who receives the fruit.

Additionally, the university will receive the following grants if the experiments are completed:

Alpha Team	Mind Expansion	$200,000
Beta Team	Birth Defects	$50,000
Charlie Team	Cancer Virus	$25,000

In addition, members of your management team have been promised bonuses for completing the experiments ahead of the 60-minute time limit, as follows:

Correct transfer of staff within:

30 minutes = $50,000

45 minutes = $30,000

55 minutes = $10,000

Each experiment completed in:

less than 30 minutes = $25,000

less than 45 minutes = $15,000

less than 55 minutes = $5,000

1. You must manage the teams' resources to obtain the largest grant consistent with the university's values and standards.

2. The number of participants per island determines the number that can be transferred to other island(s). If there are four or fewer per island, one person will have to transfer to each of the other two islands. If there are five or more per island, two will have to transfer to each of the other two islands. The teams are free to choose which member(s) should transfer.

3. The Zeno fruit may be transferred *only on the Island of Hope*. Share what you know about the Zeno fruit with the teams and help them make a decision on who should receive the Zeno. However, the teams will have the final say. You may share your bonus money with teams if you choose, but they are motivated by helping mankind and do not know that the university will receive grants for completing any of the projects.

4. An air drop has been planned for your team in 20 minutes. You may drop to the island of your choice to help with the situation there. Remember that all teams face some tough choices and are surrounded by acid. Use your own resources wisely.

RESEARCH TEAM ALPHA TASK

Your team is on a remote island as part of International University's study program of human habitation. The island is surrounded by acid and your associates are on two other remote islands also surrounded by acid. Due to poor planning, the research team members were placed on the islands in the wrong configurations, so the people with the skills needed to perform several specialized experiments must be relocated to the proper island. This transfer must occur within the next 60 minutes because no boats will return until next week, and the experiments cannot be conducted at a later time of year.

You have harvested three special, very rare Zeno fruits. Zeno skin is critical to your experiments, which have the potential to improve the utilization of the human mind by 50 percent.

Your Team's Task

Your task as a team is to transfer one or two members of your team (one if your team has four or fewer people or two if your team contains five or more) to each of the two other islands. The team as a whole should select which members will transfer. You will also be receiving new personnel from the other islands.

Remember that your island is surrounded by acid. However, the cement blocks and the barrels located on your island are protected with a special sealant. The boards are not protected, and if they touch the acid directly, they will be destroyed and your team will forfeit that board. If any team member touches the acid, he or she must return to the original starting point for decontamination.

In the middle of the three islands is an island that is safe for human habitation. If your radios are working, you will be receiving other information from home base, where the research management team is located.

Even if you can move enough of your team to the other island(s), you must have the skin of at least two more Zeno fruit to complete your experiment.

Remember:

- Jumping is not permitted!
- If any equipment is thrown, it will be considered forfeited.
- If you feel that you cannot participate for any reason, let the facilitator know.

RESEARCH TEAM BETA TASK

Your team is on a remote island as part of International University's study program of human habitation. The island is surrounded by acid and your associates are on two other remote islands also surrounded by acid. Due to poor planning, the research team members were placed on the islands in the wrong configurations, so the people with the skills needed to perform several specialized experiments must be relocated to the proper island. This transfer must occur within the next 60 minutes because no boats will return until next week, and the experiments cannot be conducted at a later time of year.

You have harvested three special, very rare Zeno fruits. Zeno seeds are critical to your experimental formula, which has the potential to cure birth defects of nearly any kind. What a breakthrough!

Your Team's Task

Your task as a team is to transfer one or two members of your team (one if your team has four or fewer people or two if your team contains five or more) to each of the two other islands. The team as a whole should select which members will transfer. You will also be receiving new personnel from the other islands.

Remember that your island is surrounded by acid. However, the cement blocks and the barrels located on your island are protected with a special sealant. The boards are not protected, and if they touch the acid directly, they will be destroyed and your team will forfeit that board. If any team member touches the acid, he or she must return to the original starting point for decontamination.

In the middle of the three islands is an island that is safe for human habitation. If your radios are working, you will be receiving other information from home base, where the research management team is located.

Even if you can move enough of your team to the other island(s), you must have the seeds of at least two more Zeno fruit to complete your experiment.

Remember:

- Jumping is not permitted!
- If any equipment is thrown, it will be considered forfeited.
- If you feel that you cannot participate for any reason, let the facilitator know.

RESEARCH TEAM CHARLIE TASK

Your team is on a remote island as part of International University's study program of human habitation. The island is surrounded by acid and your associates are on two other remote islands also surrounded by acid. Due to poor planning, the research team members were placed on the islands in the wrong configurations, so the people with the skills needed to perform several specialized experiments must be relocated to the proper island. This transfer must occur within the next 60 minutes because no boats will return until next week, and the experiments cannot be conducted at a later time of year.

You have harvested three special, very rare Zeno fruits. Zeno juice is critical to your experiments, which have the potential to eliminate all cancer in humans.

Your Team's Task

Your task as a team is to transfer one or two members of your team (one if your team has four or fewer people or two if your team contains five or more) to each of the two other islands. The team as a whole should select which members will transfer. You will also be receiving new personnel from the other islands.

Remember that your island is surrounded by acid. However, the cement blocks and the barrels located on your island are protected with a special sealant. The boards are not protected, and if they touch the acid directly, they will be destroyed and your team will forfeit that board. If any team member touches the acid, he or she must return to the original starting point for decontamination.

In the middle of the three islands is an island that is safe for human habitation. If your radios are working, you will be receiving other information from home base, where the research management team is located.

Even if you can move enough of your team to the other island(s), you must have the juice from at least four more Zeno fruit to complete your experiment.

Remember:

- Jumping is not permitted!
- If any equipment is thrown, it will be considered forfeited.
- If you feel that you cannot participate for any reason, let the facilitator know.

#39 SPY STORY

OVERVIEW

This activity uses the plot of an imaginary spy story to present intellectual and physical challenges for teams. During the first phase, each team hides a floppy disk and three secret messages specifying its location. During the second phase, each team uses the secret messages to find the floppy disk hidden by another team.

OBJECTIVES

- To create challenging puzzles for other teams to solve
- To solve challenging puzzles created by other teams
- To explore factors that influence collaboration and competition within a team
- To explore factors that influence collaboration and competition among teams

GROUP SIZE

Two to five teams of two to eight participants each

MATERIALS

- One copy each of Handouts 39.1, 39.2, and 39.3 for each team
- One copy of Handout 39.4 for the facilitator
- Paper and a pencil for each person
- Grid paper for each team
- An unlabeled floppy disk for each team
- A method for timing the initiative

SUGGESTED TIME

70 to 105 minutes (60-minute activity with a 10-minute to 45-minute debriefing)

PHYSICAL SET-UP

Indoors or outdoors, within specified boundaries, such as the first three floors of a hotel, a golf course, or a boat house and dock.

PROCEDURE

1. Organize participants into teams of two to eight participants per team.

2. Distribute copies of Handouts 39.1, 39.2, and 39.3 to each team and tell the teams that they will have 20 minutes to review the materials and solve the sample puzzles provided. Let teams work on their own to master the three puzzle formats.

3. After 20 minutes, brief the participants. Give each team an unlabeled floppy disk and say that the disk contains vital information that will affect the future of humanity. Each team should hide its disk in a secret place and create three secret messages to help another team locate it using the three puzzle formats the teams mastered earlier.

4. Explain that each team will complete the following steps during the first phase:
   - Hide the floppy disk in a secret location within the boundaries of the designated area.
   - Write a letter drop message that specifies where the disk can be found.
   - Hide the letter drop message in a different place from the floppy.
   - Create a cryptogram message that specifies the location of the letter drop message.
   - Hide the cryptogram in yet another place.
   - Finally, create a chunks message that specifies the location of the cryptogram. Teams should not hide this message, as it will be given to another team.

   > NOTE: If time is short, have teams use only one or two of the puzzle types for creating their secret message(s).

5. Encourage the teams to refer to the relevant sections of the three handouts they read earlier to construct their secret messages. Ask them to find unusual places to hide the disk and the secret messages. Announce a 20-minute time limit for this phase. Emphasize that the teams should work secretly and independently. Keep time, and give teams a 5-minute warning.

6. Stop the activity and announce that during the next phase each team will locate another team's hidden disk.

7. Have teams exchange chunks messages with one another so that every team ends up with another team's message. Tell teams to solve the chunks puzzle, use it to find the cryptogram, solve the cryptogram, and so on. Give them 20 minutes and instruct them to start.

8. When a team finds a disk, congratulate its members and ask them to help the other teams. If necessary, drop broad hints to ensure that all teams find disks within the time limit.

9. Share Handout 39.4 with everyone, then conduct a debriefing using the following questions:

   • When you were hiding the disk and creating the secret messages, did you cooperate with other members of your team or did you compete with them?

   • How did you divide up the responsibilities during the first phase of the game (when you were hiding the disk and the clues)?

   • During the first phase, did you try to make your secret messages easy or hard? Why?

   • Did your team have a leader during the first phase? Who was the leader, and how was this person chosen?

   • During the second phase, when you were solving the messages and locating a disk, did you pay attention to the progress made by the other teams? Did you feel that you were competing with the other teams?

   • How did the roles of different team members change from the first phase of the activity to the second phase? Did a new leader emerge during the second phase of the activity?

   • Did different participants have different levels of skill in constructing and solving the puzzle messages? How did this affect your behavior?

   • When the first team found its floppy, how did members of the other teams feel? Why was this so?

   • How would teams have behaved differently if they were competing to be the first to locate a disk?

   • If your team had more members, would your behavior have changed? Why do you think so?

   • If each team had a leader assigned to it, how would your behavior have changed? Why do you think so?

   • How will you use what you have learned in your current work environment?

QUOTE

"The greatest thing in the world is not so much where we stand as in which direction we are moving."

Oliver Wendell Holmes

SPY STORY CHUNKS PUZZLES

To create a chunks puzzle, take a sentence and cut it into three-character chunks (including spaces and punctuation marks). Use a rectangular box (□) to indicate the space between words. Arrange the chunks in alphabetical order.

How to Solve a Chunks Puzzle

- Locate the last chunk from the end of the sentence. This chunk will contain a period, a question mark, or an exclamation point. Work backward from this chunk, looking for other chunks that could precede it.

- Any chunk that begins with a space (□) is the beginning of a new word. Look for other chunks that could follow this chunk.

- A three-letter chunk could be a complete word (such as *and, are, the, but*) or part of a longer word. Try placing other chunks before and after the three-letter chunk.

- If a chunk ends with an apostrophe, the next letter is most likely an S (as in "let's") or a T (as in "can't"). Sometimes the apostrophe may be followed by LL (as in "we'll"), or VE (as in "I've").

- If a chunk ends with a comma or a semicolon, the next chunk should begin with a space (□).

- When you have figured out a few words, use the context to suggest additional words. For example, if one of the words is *play,* you may find the word *game* somewhere in the sentence.

- You may cut out the chunks and physically move them around. If you don't want to cut the original puzzle, make a photocopy and cut the copy instead.

- You can also work out the solution on a separate piece of paper, writing down different words and phrases and rearranging them into a sentence later. Put a mark next to the chunks that you have already incorporated into your partial solution.

- Work with a partner or a team. It's amazing how different perspectives can speed up the process of solving the puzzle.

The next page contains a chunks puzzle. To solve a chunks puzzle, rearrange the chunks to form a sentence.

CAN

EET

E□M

HE□

□IN

ING

K□U

LOO

NDE

OM.

□RO

R□T

SH□

□TH

TRA

How to Create a Chunks Message

1. Write your message, using uppercase letters throughout. The best length for the message is thirty-five to fifty characters (including spaces and punctuation marks).

   LOOK UNDER THE TRASH CAN IN THE MEETING ROOM.

2. Insert a rectangular box to indicate spaces between words. This prevents you from ignoring them later.

   LOOK□UNDER□THE□TRASH□CAN□IN□THE□MEETING□ROOM.

3. Draw vertical lines to divide the message into three-character chunks. Be sure to include spaces and punctuation marks.

   LOO|K□U|NDE|R□T|HE□|TRA|SH□|CAN|□IN|□TH|E□M|EET|ING|□RO|OM.|

4. Copy the chunks in alphabetical order on a separate piece of paper.

   CAN

   EET

   E□M

   HE□

   □IN

   ING

   K□U

   LOO

   NDE

   OM.

   □RO

   R□T

   SH□

   □TH

   TRA

SPY STORY CRYPTOGRAMS

You are probably familiar with codes, ciphers, and cryptograms. In a cryptogram, each letter in the message is replaced by another letter of the alphabet. For example, LET THE GAMES BEGIN may become this cryptogram: YZF FOZ JUKZH CZJVQ. In the cryptogram Y replaces L, Z replaces E, F replaces T, and so on. Notice that the same letter substitutions are used throughout this cryptogram: Every E in the sentence is replaced by a Z, and every T is replaced by an F.

How to Solve a Cryptogram

Letter Frequency

- The most commonly used letters of the English language are *e, t, a, I, o, n, s, h,* and *r.*
- The letters that are most commonly found at the beginning of words are *t, a, o, d,* and *w.*
- The letters that are most commonly found at the end of words are *e, s, d,* and *t.*

Word Frequency

- Short words provide useful clues. One-letter words are either *a* or *I.*
- The most common two-letter words are *an, as, at, be, by, do, he, if, in, is, it, my, of, on, or, so, to, up,* and *we.*
- The most common three-letter words are *all, and, any, are, but, for, had, has, her, his, for, man, not, one, out, the, was,* and *you.*
- The most common four-letter words are *been, from, good, have, much, some, that, they, this, very, want, will, with,* and *your.*

Word Endings

- The most common word endings are *-able, -ance, -ed, -ent, -ight, -ing, -ion, -ist, -ment, -ous,* and *-tion.*

Doubled Letters

- The most frequent double-letter combinations are *cc, ee, ff, ll, nn, oo, pp, rr, ss,* and *tt.*
- The double letters that occur most commonly at the end of words are *ee, ff, ll,* and *ss.*

Punctuation

- A comma is often followed by *and, but,* or *who.*
- A question often begins with *did, how, was, what, where, which, who,* or *why.*
- Two words that often precede quotation marks are *said* and *says.*
- Two letters that usually follow an apostrophe are *t* and *s.*

How to Create a Cryptogram

1. Write the letters of the alphabet on a piece of paper:

   ABCDEFGHIJKLMNOPQRSTUVWXYZ

2. Select a key word. This word should be at least five letters long and should not have any duplicate letters. For example, QUICKLY, SHORTEN, and MOUSE are appropriate key words. Longer words are better, but make sure there are no repeated letters.

3. Write the key word under the alphabet line you wrote earlier. Line up the letters in the key word with the letters in the alphabet.

   ABCDEFGHIJKLMNOPQRSTUVWXYZ

   QUICKLY

4. Write the remaining letters of the alphabet after your key word. When you come to a letter that is in your key word, skip it.

   ABCDEFGHIJKLMNOPQRSTUVWXYZ

   QUICKLYABDEFGHJMNOPRSTVWXZ

5. Write your message in plain text. The longer the message, the easier it will be to solve. For each letter in the message that appears on the alphabet line (see #4 above), substitute the letter from the line below.

   LOOK UNDER THE TRASH CAN IN THE MEETING ROOM.

   FJJE SHCKO RAK ROQPA IQH BH RAK GKKRBHY OJJG.

6. Copy the encrypted message on a piece of paper.

Sample Cryptogram

See whether you can solve the following cryptogram by using repeated letters and patterns of letters in the words. There is space between the lines for you to write the solution.

RTN CVMM KVQE AJY QYOA FYXXDZY VQ

AJY SJTQY LTTAJ. AJY FYXXDZY VX

ADSYE AT AJY LTAATF TK AJY SJTQY.

SPY STORY LETTER DROP PUZZLES

A letter drop puzzle is created in a grid in which the goal is to determine the correct order and arrangement of the letters provided. Remember three important things about the layout of the puzzle:

1. Letters in each column are to be placed in the boxes beneath them.
2. Black boxes indicate a space between words. If the end of the line does not have a black box, the word is continued at the beginning of the next line.
3. Punctuation marks are already in the appropriate boxes.

How to Solve a Letter Drop Puzzle

The following hints will help you solve letter drop puzzles:

- Use a pencil with an eraser. It is a trial-and-error activity.
- Be systematic in your work. Whenever you write a letter in an empty box, be sure to cross it out from the column above.
- Do not try to work from the beginning to the end. Keep jumping from one word to another.
- Begin with one-letter words. They will be either *a* or *I*.
- Two-letter words are also easy to figure out. They are usually prepositions such as *in*, *of*, *on*, and *to*. The words *it* and *is* also appear frequently.
- Three-letter words can sometimes be solved easily. Try the words *and*, *but*, or *the*.
- Long words can be easy to solve. Look at the letters in the columns above and try different combinations.
- It is sometimes easy to guess the ending of a long word. Try such suffixes as *-able*, *-ed*, *-ies*, *-ing*, *-ion*, *ive*, and *-tion*.
- If there is only one letter in a column, simply copy it to the correct box.
- Look at the letters available before and after a letter you have already guessed. Certain letters can be eliminated because they do not form usable combinations. For example, you cannot have the combination *pk* or *qz*.
- When you have a few words identified, use the context to provide you with additional suggestions. For example, if one of the words is *man*, you may find the word *he* somewhere in the sentence.

How to Create a Letter Drop Puzzle

1. Write a message, using uppercase letters throughout. The best length for the message is thirty-five to forty-five characters (including punctuation marks and spaces).

LOOK UNDER THE TRASH CAN IN THE MEETING ROOM.

2. On a piece of grid paper, mark off an area fifteen squares wide. Copy the message onto the square you have marked, one letter, punctuation mark, or space per square. When you reach the end of the line, continue on the next line, breaking words as they fall.

LOOK UNDER THE

TRASH CAN IN TH

E MEETING ROOM.

3. Count the number of lines. On another piece of grid paper, mark off an area fifteen squares wide and *twice* as many lines high. Draw a horizontal line between the top and bottom halves of your area.

4. In the bottom half, write the punctuation marks in the corresponding squares. Blacken the squares that correspond to spaces in the message, as well as the squares past the end of the message.

5. Look at the message in the area you marked off. Look at the columns of the message. Take the letters in the first column, alphabetize them, and write them in the squares in the first column of the top half.

6. Repeat this process for the remaining columns. Study the sample below, then try to solve the puzzle on the next page.

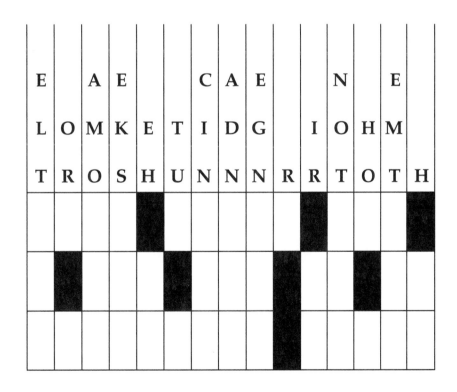

Sample Letter Drop Puzzle

To solve the letter drop puzzle below, move each letter to one of the empty boxes below it. Do not put any letters in the black boxes. If you place all the letters in the correct boxes, you will spell out a message, reading from left to right and top to bottom.

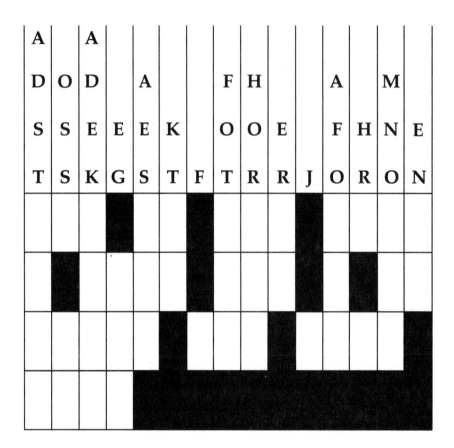

SPY STORY SOLUTIONS

Chunks Message
Look under the rock next to the oldest oak tree.

Cryptogram
You will find the next message in the phone booth. The message is taped to the bottom of the phone.

Letter Drop Puzzle (page 210)

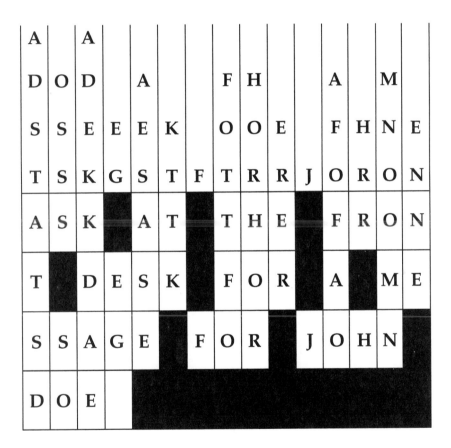

#40 OPERATION PVC

OVERVIEW

Team members must transport marbles inside PVC tubes from Point A to Point B on a course with obstacles; the details of transport are left to the team's creativity. Each participant assists with the transport, but is not permitted to move when touching the tube containing the marbles. If any participant drops the marbles, the entire team loses the ability to communicate verbally.

OBJECTIVES

- To solve a task using creative thinking
- To complete a task using cooperation between team members
- To complete a task under pressure and time constraints
- To permit team members to put their theories of team problem solving into action

GROUP SIZE

Five to thirty participants in teams of up to ten members, ideally five

MATERIALS

- One 12-inch piece of ¾-inch PVC tube per participant
- Five marbles per team
- One copy of Handout 40.1 for the facilitator
- A copy of Handout 40.2 for each team
- A method for timing the initiative

PHYSICAL SET-UP

Indoors or outdoors with plenty of space to accommodate the number of teams chosen

SUGGESTED TIME

40 minutes (20-minute activity with 20-minute debriefing)

PROCEDURE

1. Cut ¾-inch PVC tubing into 12-inch lengths, with the ends cut at different angles to make it difficult to align the tube ends. Do not cut the ends straight. (*Option:* Use ½-inch PVC tubes along with ¾-inch tubes to add additional difficulty.)

2. Prior to the activity, select where the participants will begin (Point A) and where they will finish (Point B). Also choose any obstacles you want to place between these two points.

> *NOTE:* If you do select obstacles, be sure to provide appropriate spotting during this activity.

3. Copy Handout 40.2 in advance and place a copy into an envelope for each team so that the team members can open it and plan their strategy without your direction or help. Your role is to provide clarification only.

4. When the group meets, divide the members into teams of five if possible. Be sure to compare the dynamics of different size teams during the debriefing, if that is possible.

5. When ready to begin, place the PVC tubes on the floor. Tell the participants that they can select their own tubes.

6. Give each team an envelope containing the handout and direct the members to open the envelope and read it. (This duplicates the real experience of data coming to a team and their subsequent utilization of this data.)

7. After the teams have finished reading Handout 40.2, tell them that successful marble transport companies complete similar tasks in under 20 minutes. Stress that if they fail, their entire company could be out of business in a short period of time.

8. Identify points A and B only after team members request the information.

9. Determine the order in which teams will attempt the task.

10. Load the marbles in one of the first team's PVC tubes. Tell the teams that once you hand the tube off, if any of the marbles fall out, the team will be penalized by not being allowed to talk.

11. Do not volunteer information. Make team members ask questions in order to obtain it.

12. After all of the teams have completed (or at least attempted) the task, conduct a debriefing session using the following questions:
    * How successful was your team?
    * What problems did your team experience?
    * Can you identify specific behaviors that helped your team?
    * What behaviors had a negative effect on the team?
    * How was the leadership role handled by your team?
    * How were individual ideas processed? Explain.

- Did team members support one another?
- Did any "out-of-box" thinking occur?
- What would you do differently if you were faced with this challenge again?
- How would you relate this experience to day-to-day operation in your company?
- What learning can you take from this experience to make you a better team member in the future?

QUOTE

"A business is a reflection of a leader. A fish doesn't stink just from the tail, and a company doesn't succeed or fail from the bottom."

Gary Feldmar

OPERATION PVC SOLUTION

There is no right or wrong way to complete this task; however, many teams have been extremely successful using only two tubes—one containing the marbles and the other securing the marbles inside the carrying tube, preventing them from falling out, as illustrated below:

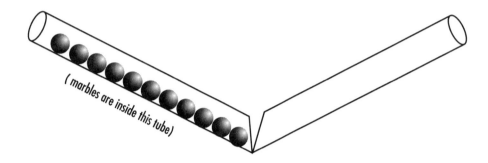

(marbles are inside this tube)

   This technique allows the structure to be passed from person to person, rather than rolling the marbles down the many tubes. Remember, only the person holding the tube with the marbles cannot move his or her feet.
   There are most likely other variations yet to be discovered.

OPERATION PVC TEAM TASK

Your team must transport five marbles from Point A to Point B with the following constraints:

- No one may touch the marbles; the facilitator will load the first person's tube when your team is ready.

- If a marble is dropped, all members lose the ability to speak!

- When you are touching the tube containing the marbles you cannot move your feet.

- No material except the PVC tubing can touch the marbles.

- You may not carry teammates, nor can you wheel or push a teammate in a chair.

- If the tubes are of two different sizes, placing the smaller tubes inside the larger ones is not permitted.

- You have 20 minutes to complete this task.

#41 HULA HOOPS

OVERVIEW

A team must move a hula hoop around a circle while members hold hands. Another hula hoop is then added to the circle, and the team must move it around the circle in the opposite direction. This event is timed, and the team must attempt to reduce their time and make improvements. Emphasis is on continual improvement and group dynamics.

OBJECTIVES

- To demonstrate the dynamics of processing various inputs within a team environment
- To allow participants to experience problem solving in a group
- To allow participants to get to know one another better in a fun and interesting way
- To seek continuous improvement
- To experience various group-processing dynamics

GROUP SIZE

Ten to twelve people per circle with no more than two groups per facilitator

MATERIALS

- One large Hula Hoop for every group of ten or twelve participants
- One slightly smaller Hula Hoop (so it can pass through the larger one) for each ten or twelve participants

NOTE: Be sure to verify the sizes when you purchase the Hula Hoops.

- A method for timing the initiative

PHYSICAL SET-UP

Outdoors or indoors if there is enough room for the circles

SUGGESTED TIME

40 to 60 minutes (20-minute to 30-minute activity with 20-minute to 30-minute debriefing)

PROCEDURE

1. Divide the participants into groups of ten to twelve members each.

2. Ask each team to form a circle holding hands.

3. Ask one person in each group to let go of the hand of the person next to him or her. Put the larger of the two Hula Hoops over that person's arm and have the two people rejoin hands.

4. Explain that the team's task is to pass the hoop to the right, around the entire circle. Let each group do that once to get the feel of it.

5. Now ask a different person on each team to let go of the hand of the person next to him or her. Place the second (smaller) Hula Hoop over that person's arm and have the people rejoin hands.

6. Tell the teams that their new task is to move this new hoop to the left while moving the other one to the right. Tell the teams you will time them.

7. Time how long it takes each group to get both hula hoops around the circle and back to their starting points. Inform the teams of their times and ask if they can improve. Allow time for them to discuss and implement improvements.

8. Go through this process several times.

9. After each group is satisfied that it cannot improve on its time, conduct a debriefing session using the following questions:

   • What was your initial reaction to the task?
   • How did your team handle team member inputs?
   • How did your team decide on whose suggestions to implement?
   • What behaviors did you feel good about on your team?
   • What behaviors did you feel could be improved?
   • What was the ultimate required behavior to solve the problem?
   • In what ways does this experience parallel your current work environment?
   • What insights can you take back to your day-to-day job environment?

QUOTE

"It's not so much what happens to us, as what happens in us that counts, or what we think has happened to us."

Tim Hansel

#42   ATROC

OVERVIEW

Participants are separated into "departments" responsible for saving a company through problem solving and teamwork. Each department must solve four out of the five problems presented to it within the current fiscal year, which ends in 15 minutes.

OBJECTIVES

- To discover the benefits of working together as a team
- To use the ATROC behaviors—adaptability, trustworthiness, resourcefulness, optimism, and consideration
- To realize that individuals sometimes place restrictions on themselves that block their success

GROUP SIZE

Ten to forty people, depending on the experience of the facilitator, room size, and group dynamics, divided into teams of two to six people each

MATERIALS

- A copy of Handout 42.1 for each team
- One 3-foot piece of rope for each team
- One "T" puzzle for each team
- Six toothpicks for each team
- A copy of Figure 42.1 for the facilitator
- A copy of Handout 42.2 for the facilitator to share with participants at the close of the session
- A method for timing the initiative

PHYSICAL SET-UP

Indoors in a conference or training room with separate areas for the groups

SUGGESTED TIME

45 minutes (20-minute activity with a 25-minute debriefing)
(Groups of more than twenty will probably require additional time for debriefing.)

PROCEDURE

1. Prepare puzzle pieces in advance using index stock or heavy construction paper according to the dimensions shown in Figure 42.1. Place each puzzle in an envelope.

2. Inform the participants that they are going to learn first-hand about team dynamics and have some fun while doing so.

3. Separate the participants into "departments" with two to six people in each. The goal is to create a traditional company structure.

> NOTE: It is better to have four departments with two in each department than two departments with four people in each.

4. Provide each department with a piece of rope, six toothpicks, and the envelope with the puzzle in it.

5. Separate the departments as well as possible based on the space available.

6. Tell each department to select a "department manager" and ask that person to report to the "plant manager" (the facilitator).

7. Conduct a meeting with department managers, stressing the importance of solving problems. Emphasize that they must "produce." Mention that "everyone is in this together," but don't emphasize this too much. Distribute a copy of Handout 42.1 to each department manager. Make sure they understand their tasks and that they must complete these tasks within the 15-minute time constraint.

> NOTE: The idea is for plant managers to conduct meetings with their "employees" to inform them of the problem and what must be accomplished to save the company. Most likely, they will go back to their groups and continue as individual departments with separate goals. The point is that if the company fails, then they all fail, yet teams will display destructive, competitive behaviors.

8. While you are meeting with the departmental managers, the department members should occupy themselves as real employees would do without directions.

9. After the department managers return to their departments, instruct the teams to begin the activity.

10. Check on each group regularly, asking how things are going, if the department will meet the schedule, or if they need any help. If teams do ask for help, you may choose to give them hints, but do not disclose the answers.

11. Observe each department, noting specific behaviors that help or hinder teamwork and the problem-solving process.

12. Stop the activity after 15 minutes regardless of the number of problems each team has solved.

13. Go from department to department, asking each one to present as many answers as the group was able to solve.

14. Ask each department to answer the following questions while still in a separate area:

    - Were you successful as a team?
    - How did you define your team?
    - How would you rate your teamwork on a scale of 1 to 10, with 10 being high?
    - What did you do well?
    - What could be improved?
    - How did the department manager affect your behavior?

15. Next, reconvene the entire group and review the responses you received from each team to the questions above.

16. Make everyone aware that this activity was assigned to the whole company, not just to individual departments.

17. Once the participants realize that they were all striving for the same goal, ask them if that awareness changes their answers to the questions above.

18. Explain the ATROC behaviors to the participants and ask them to give examples of when they used these behaviors.

19. Ask the participants: "What can be learned from this experience that will benefit your future team project(s)?"

20. Review the answers from Handout 42.2 with the participants at the end of the session. Do not forget this part of the initiative!

QUOTE

"The hallmark of a well-managed organization is not the absence of problems, but whether or not problems are effectively resolved."

Steve Ventura

Figure 42.1. T Puzzle Instructions

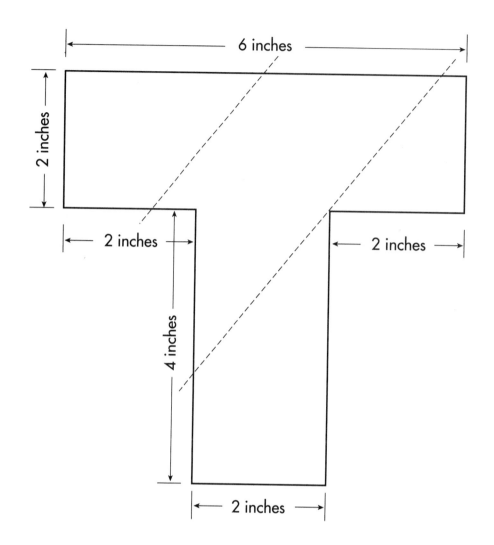

ATROC TEAM GOALS

Your department has the following fiscal year goals:

- Solve four of the following five problems during the remainder of this fiscal year (which ends in 15 minutes).

- All department managers should submit their answers to the plant manager (the facilitator) at the end of this fiscal year.

Your plant manager has delivered the following message:

"Our competitors have already solved these problems, and for us to be successful as a company, we must find the answers. Good luck in your problem solving."

Problems

1. Create four equilateral triangles with the six toothpicks provided.

2. Every person on the team must be able to hold the ends of the rope and, without letting go, tie a knot in the rope.

3. Form the four pieces in the envelope into the letter T.

4. A man was walking in a country unfamiliar to him. He came to a crossroads where he found that the signpost had fallen over. How did he find out which way to go?

5. Three men went into a diner and each had a single cup of coffee. Each put an odd number of lumps of sugar into his coffee. In total, they put 12 lumps into their cups. How many lumps did each add?

ATROC SOLUTION SHEET

1. *Toothpick Solution:* Think in terms of 3-D!

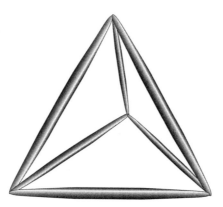

2. *Rope Solution:* The key here is to break your paradigm and fold your arms before grabbing the ends of the rope. When you pull your arms apart, a knot will form.

3. *The T-Puzzle Solution:* The T puzzle has been around for many years, but people still have problems with it. See Figure 42.1 for the layout of the puzzle and the solution.

4. *Fallen Sign Solution:* If the man puts the sign back up with the appropriate marking or arrow facing the direction he came from, then the other directions will be correct.

5. *Sugar Lump Solution:* 1, 1, and 10. The 1s are odd numbers, and 10 lumps of sugar is certainly a *very odd* number to put into a cup of coffee.

#43 HEARTS WARS*

OVERVIEW

Each team must maximize its profit. Teams identify themselves with a suit—spades, clubs, or diamonds, and select a leader to negotiate selections with other teams. Teams earn points based on their card's face or number. Each team's aim should be to obtain 30 points in heart face cards.

OBJECTIVES

- To experience the effects of leadership on a team
- To demonstrate various dynamics of leader selection
- To illustrate the role of cooperation in today's work environments
- To demonstrate the importance of consideration for others

GROUP SIZE

Three teams with three to five members on each

MATERIALS

- One deck of regular playing cards for every three teams playing

PHYSICAL SET-UP

Indoors with round tables so that all participants can see the cards as they are played

SUGGESTED TIME

60 to 75 minutes (30-minute to 45-minute activity with a 30-minute debriefing)

_____

*This is an adaptation of an original idea by Dick Teach at Georgia Tech.

PROCEDURE

1. Prior to the activity, separate each deck of cards into hearts, diamonds, spades, and clubs.

2. Form the participants into three teams. You may allow them to do this on their own or you can select team members based on your objectives for the day.

3. Give each of the three teams a suit of cards, either diamonds, spades, or clubs. Keep the hearts for yourself.

4. Explain that participants will be playing a game in which the objective is to win 30 points worth of hearts.

5. Give the following guidelines:

   • Each team will select a team member to make the decision about when to play a card. He or she will be the team leader.

   • A team receives points each time it wins the hand, that is, plays the card with the highest value (Ace = 14, King = 13, Queen = 12, Jack = 11, 10 = 10 and so on).

   • The number of points awarded for each hand is equal to the value of the heart cards won during that round.

   • Participants may talk to members of other teams only before play starts.

   • No one may talk during a hand.

   • Teams may not give their cards to other teams once they have won them.

6. Encourage team leaders to negotiate with one another prior to the beginning of the game (only if they do not do this on their own).

7. Begin the game by selecting a heart and playing it face up. Tell the leaders to select their first cards and to place their selections face down on the table.

8. Instruct the team leaders to turn their cards over. The team with the highest value card wins the round and counts the number of points represented by the heart card.

9. Continue on in this manner for four more cards.

10. After you play the fifth card, allow team leaders to confer with their team members and discuss their progress. The teams leaders can also discuss progress with the other team leaders. The objective is to let the teams figure out that if they work together they can all meet the goal of obtaining 30 points. There is no benefit to them to get more than 30 points. If they fight with one another, one or more teams may lose; but if they collaborate, they will all meet their goals.

> NOTE: If you plan to play two rounds, then do not break during the first round. Wait until the second round to allow teams to confer.

11. After a few minutes, tell the teams it is time to start again and play the remaining eight cards.

12. After all the cards have been played, total up the number of heart points for each team.

13. Conduct a debriefing session using the following questions:

- (If the teams selected their own members) How did you select your team members? What criteria did you base the selection on?

- How did your team select its leader?

- What goals did your team decide on?

- Did your team discuss the overall task?

- Who decided on the strategy? The team or leader?

- Did your team leader negotiate with other team leaders?

- How did you feel as a team member? Did you feel that your role was limited?

- Were there any attempts to cooperate with the other teams?

- Did any team members disagree with their leader? If so, did they communicate this to the leader?

- In what ways does this experience parallel your current work environment?

- What insights can you take back to your day-to-day job environment?

QUOTE

"Coaching isn't an addition to a [leader's] job, it's an integral part of it."

George Odiorne

#44 RECOGNIZING EACH TEAM MEMBER*

OVERVIEW

At the end of a team-building session, participants present a token of appreciation to other team members.

OBJECTIVES

- To allow team members to feel appreciated for their accomplishments during the session
- To begin the process of open recognition that helps develop team culture
- To end the session on a productive, synergistic note

GROUP SIZE

Any number of participants

MATERIALS

- Some tokens (T-shirts, pens, hats, trophies, key chains, or other items) for members to present to one another

PHYSICAL SET-UP

Indoors or outdoors

SUGGESTED TIME

Varies, depending on the energy of the group

---

*Adapted from an original concept by Jeff Boyd, Operation Explore.

PROCEDURE

1. At the end of a team-building session, bring the group together in a circle so that all members can make eye contact with one another.

2. Tell the group you have some tokens for them to hand out. Ask for a volunteer to present the first token to another member. Tell people to select one of the items and to present it to one of the other group members in recognition of something that person did during the session that the presenter appreciated or noticed.

3. The person giving the token should articulate this appreciation as he or she hands the token to the other person. (This process may start off slowly.)

4. Say that a person may receive only one token, but that each presenter may give as many as desired. Encourage all to participate in the presentation, but do not force those who do not want to be involved.

5. An optional debriefing may be conducted using the following questions:

   - What have you learned from this team-building experience?
   - What is the one thing you will take away from this session for future use in life? On the job?
   - Has your viewpoint on the initiatives changed in any way during this session?
   - What behaviors do you think help a team become truly successful?
   - In what ways does this experience parallel your current work environment?
   - What insights can you take back to your day-to-day job environment?

QUOTE

"It's not what is said that's important, it's how it's said that matters."

Ed Rose

#45 THREE WARM-UP ACTIVITIES

OVERVIEW

Some short activities are included here that help a group to loosen up and prepare to focus on the initiatives or group functions at hand.

SHARING

Overview

A short activity that encourages discussion among the group members, focusing on starting off on a positive note.

Objectives

- To open up discussion about the similarities among people
- To allow participants to communicate in a nonthreatening environment
- To set the stage for what might be more difficult topics to come

Group Size

Any number

Materials

None

Physical Set-Up

Indoors or outside

Suggested Time

Dependant on group size and the time available, as well as the interest and energy level of the group

Procedure

1. Ask each participant to share with the group a good thing that happened recently.

2. Then ask each participant to share a good thing that someone else did for them recently.

3. Next ask each participant to share something good he or she did for someone else recently.

4. Lead a debriefing session using the following questions:

   - What can we determine from some of these examples?

   - Are people generally concerned about the same things?

   - Do people generally help others?

   - How do you feel when you help other people?

   - Should we always look for something in return?

   - What can we learn from some of the stories we have heard today?

A SIMPLE TASK

Overview

A short activity to involve the group in your presentation that can be applied for many different subjects.

Objectives

- To warm up the participants
- To allow participants to explore problems in communication

Group Size

Ten to one hundred

Materials

- A method for timing the initiative

Physical Set-Up

Inside, with enough chairs for each participant

Suggested Time

25 minutes (5-minute activity with a 20-minute debriefing)

Procedure

1. Inform the participants that they must improve their seating order within 2 minutes, but do not give them any further instructions.
2. Tell the participants to begin.
3. Stop the activity after 2 minutes.
4. Ask the participants to explain in what way they improved the seating order.
5. Debrief the activity using the following questions:
   - Did you receive a clear goal?
   - Did you understand your goal?
   - Did you seek clarification?
   - What happened when you asked for clarification?
   - How can you relate this experience to your work environment?
   - Have you ever received a task like this before?
   - How can we prevent this type of poor communication during our session today?

UNDERSTANDING EMOTIONS

Overview

Participants demonstrate nonverbally what an emotion of their choosing looks like.

Objectives

- To use the imagination for demonstrative purposes
- To begin discussion about the effects of emotions
- To demonstrate the role of body language in communication

Group Size

Ten to thirty

Materials

- A flip chart
- Felt-tipped markers

Physical Set-Up

A room large enough to hold all of the participants comfortably

Suggested Time

10 to 20 minutes (5-minute to 10-minute activity with a 5-minute to 10-minute debriefing)

Procedure

1. Ask participants to name the various emotions humans experience, such as happiness, sadness, anger, confusion, and so forth.

2. Write each emotion on the flip chart. Continue until the participants run out of emotions.

3. Ask each participant to select an emotion listed and to demonstrate what it looks like nonverbally.

4. After everyone has had a chance to display an emotion, ask them what effects these emotions have on teamwork. Record these effects on the flip chart.

5. Conduct a debriefing session using the following questions:
   - How can you change the negative effects of emotions?
   - What role does body language play in communication?
   - In what ways does this experience parallel your current work environment?
   - What insights can you take back to your day-to-day job environment?

QUOTE

"When people work in a place that cares about them, they contribute a lot more than duty."
Dennis Hayes

#46 TAG! YOU'RE IT!

OVERVIEW

This activity is designed to be a warm up or icebreaker. Participants play three games of tag, but with a small twist. This seems silly to most participants when they start, but the benefits are great.

> *NOTE:* The three tag exercises presented here are most effective when used together in order, as they build on one another.

OBJECTIVES

- To allow participants to transition from where they are to the day's activities
- To provide a fun activity that everyone can relate to

GROUP SIZE

Ten to twenty participants

MATERIALS

- A 50-foot length of rope
- Tennis ball or bandanna

PHYSICAL SET-UP

Outside

SUGGESTED TIME

15 minutes

PROCEDURE

1. Bring participants together in a circle. Mark the circle (with rope, if available) to define the playing area. The diameter of the circle will vary according to your group. The object is to make this initiative challenging, but not too difficult.

2. Ask the participants if any of them has ever played tag before.

> NOTE: At this point, some of the group may smile a little and some may think to themselves that this is silly. Continue without discussion.

3. Tell the participants that after you explain the rules, if any participants cannot participate due to a physical constraint, that it is alright.

4. Begin Game 1: Walking Tag
   - Ask the participants to form pairs.
   - Instruct the pairs to select one partner to be "it" to start.
   - The person who is "it" stands still and counts "1001, 1002, 1003," then sets out to tag his or her partner.
   - Tell the participants that they will switch roles as in the normal game of tag.
   - Instruct the participants that they must walk not run, and that they cannot leave the circle.
   - End this activity when you see people's energy levels declining.

5. Begin Game 2: Hug Tag
   - Ask for a volunteer or select one person to be "it." Give that person a ball or bandanna to hold, signifying that he or she is "it." The person who is it must tag someone else and give him or her the ball or bandanna in order to make that person become "it."
   - Tell the remaining participants that they can find safety in groupings of three: three people touching one another cannot be tagged. Refer to this as a "hug." Explain that there must only be three people to a hug. More than three invalidates the hug and any and all are eligible to be tagged. Inform participants that they cannot remain in hugs throughout the entire game. A hug should be formed to avoid being tagged, then must break up.
   - End this activity when you see people's energy level declining.

> NOTE: This game seems to go over best with mixed gender groups.

6. Begin Game 3: Last Person Standing/All for Themselves Tag
   - Tell the participants that *everyone* is "it."
   - Instruct the participants that when you say "Go," they are free to try to tag someone else.
   - When someone is tagged, that person must kneel down. Those people are out of the game.
   - The last person standing will be the winner.
   - No diving or jumping is allowed. Play safe!
7. No debriefing questions are recommended for this activity, which is basically effective for warming up groups before other initiatives.

QUOTE

"The most important quality in a leader is that of being acknowledged as such."

Andre Maurois

#47 THE BLINDFOLD SQUARES

OVERVIEW

The participants are divided into two subgroups and asked to form two overlapping squares while blindfolded.

OBJECTIVES

- To allow participants to experience intra-group and inter-group communication
- To perform under pressure with limited information
- To allow participants to experience the power of a shared vision in organizations

GROUP SIZE

A minimum of eight participants, but this activity also works well with groups of twenty to forty

MATERIALS

- One blindfold for each participant
- Two 30-foot pieces of ½-inch nylon rope
- A method for timing the initiative

PHYSICAL SET-UP

Indoors or outdoors in a large unobstructed space for participants to move around

SUGGESTED TIME

60 to 75 minutes (30-minute activity with a 30-minute to 45-minute debriefing)

PROCEDURE

1. Before the start of the activity, choose an unobstructed area with enough space for participants to move around comfortably.

2. Have the participants form two groups of roughly equal size, and hand out a blindfold to each participant. The groups may be allowed to elect a leader at this stage if desired.

3. Tell the participants that they will be blindfolded during the initiative, but that they will be allowed to talk with one another and with the other group.

> NOTE: If any participant feels uncomfortable at any time during the activity because of the blindfold, allow him or her to remove it for awhile to become oriented and then put the blindfold back on. If any participant does not want to wear a blindfold, he or she can still participate, but will not be allowed to talk.

4. Have the participants put on their blindfolds.

5. Once blindfolded, each group will be led by you to the place where the initiative is to be conducted. A second facilitator/observer should be utilized to lead the second group simultaneously while you take the first group. If a second facilitator/observer is not available, instruct the second group to remain still while you lead the first group to the location, and then come back to lead the second group. Participants are to walk in single file and place their hands on the shoulders of the person in front of them.

6. Once both groups are in place, instruct each group to form a circle by holding hands. Then drop one piece of rope in the center of each circle.

7. Instruct participants to retrieve the piece of rope from the center of the circle and use it to help them form a square, and then to merge with the other group's square such that the overlap of the two squares is approximately 25 percent.

8. Inform them that they have exactly 30 minutes to accomplish the task.

9. Have the participants begin.

10. When the task is successfully completed (or the 30 minutes have expired), conduct a debriefing session using the following questions:

    • What went well for each group in forming its own square? What went badly?

    • Why was it difficult making the two groups' squares overlap by 25 percent?

    • What did you learn about communicating with one another and with other groups when we cannot see them?

    • What are necessary factors that must be in place for the two groups to do the job?

    • How is this situation like your workplace?

QUOTE

"Where there is no vision, the people perish."

Proverbs 29:18

#48 CREATIVE BALLOONS

OVERVIEW

This activity is intended as a warm up. Each individual is given a balloon to inflate. The group then must create a design with all of their balloons that represents them as a unit.

OBJECTIVES

- To emphasize the importance of teamwork
- To use imagination and personal creativity to create something artistic

GROUP SIZE

Unlimited, with a minimum of 20

MATERIALS

- One creative balloon—the type used by clowns to make funny designs or animals—per participant

PHYSICAL SET-UP

Indoors in a room with enough round tables and chairs to accommodate all of the participants

SUGGESTED TIME

15 to 20 minutes, depending on group size

PROCEDURE

1. Ask the participants to be seated at any of the tables. Tell the participants that each table represents a team.

2. Give a balloon to each person at each table.

3. Ask them to blow up the balloons and form a design from all the balloons at their table that represents their team or the focus of the session.

4. If music is available, play it, because it adds atmosphere to the initiative. If you do use music, be sure to attend to any copyright issues.

5. After each of the teams has completed the initial part of the task, have all teams gather together around one of the tables. Make sure at least one representative from each team is seated at the table. Remaining participants may stand around the table.

6. Begin another design session with all of the participants this time. Instruct the participants to join all of the designs together into one big design representing the entire group.

7. Display the design during the remainder of the session to represent the group.

8. Debrief using the following questions:

   - How does this activity relate to teamwork?

   - How did you process team members' ideas?

   - Did any conflicts develop?

   - What behaviors did your team members exhibit that you appreciated?

QUOTE

"Being powerful is like being a lady. If you have to tell people you are, you aren't."

Margaret Thatcher

#49 THE FINAL DEBRIEFING

OVERVIEW

This activity is designed to be conducted at the end of a full-day training session. Participants are separated into teams and instructed to recall key learning points and inputs from the various debriefing sessions of the day. Each team then discusses and selects five key learning points to present to the whole group. The teams select a representative to present their findings to the group, and each representative explains to the group why these key points are important and how they can enhance teamwork back in the workplace.

OBJECTIVES

- To transfer the day's learning experiences from the collective initiatives back to the work environment
- To recall inputs and key learning points from each debriefing session that may help the participants become more successful

GROUP SIZE

No limit

MATERIALS

- A flip chart for each team
- Felt-tipped markers
- A method for timing the initiative

PHYSICAL SET-UP

Indoors or outdoors wherever seating is available

SUGGESTED TIME

45 to 90 minutes, depending on group energy and the length of the session being debriefed

PROCEDURE

1. If possible, have the group separate into four teams. Give each team a flip chart and markers.

2. Instruct each team to brainstorm a list of key learning points or inputs from the day's session and to record them on a flip chart.

3. Direct each team to select five learning points or inputs that were the most important. Tell the teams that they should focus on what they have learned from this experience that will produce positive behavioral changes back in the workplace.

4. After teams have worked on their lists and selected the five most important points, ask each team to select a representative to explain to the entire group why these learning points will positively influence their teamwork on the job.

5. Allow the teams 15 minutes to prepare their presentations.

6. After 15 minutes, each team representative should present his or her team's findings to the group.

7. After the team presentations, ask the entire group to decide on the five key learning points that they can focus on and apply to their workplaces.

QUOTE

"None of us is as smart as all of us."

Peter Grazier

#50 IT'S ALL IN YOUR VISION

OVERVIEW

Participants perform a physical activity to demonstrate the power of visualization.

OBJECTIVES

- To demonstrate that visualization is of value for individual and group success
- To provide a warm-up activity for a session on positive attitudes

GROUP SIZE

No limit

MATERIALS

None

PHYSICAL SET-UP

Outdoors or indoors, with enough room for participants to spread their arms

SUGGESTED TIME

15 minutes (5-minute activity with a 10-minute debriefing)

PROCEDURE

1. Explain to the group that you would like to assist them with an activity that demonstrates the power of visualization.
2. Ask the group to spread out so they have enough room to move their arms.
3. Advise them to stand with both feet spread apart about shoulder width. Everyone should be comfortable.

4. Ask participants to raise their left arms, and demonstrate by turning your back to the group how to hold their palms forward with their fingers and thumb aligned.

5. Tell them to sight down their arms as though they were hunters with a rifle, then to rotate their bodies to the right, without moving their feet, as far as they can. Have the participants make a mental note of where they stopped.

6. Now ask them to return to their original positions and follow your directions.

7. It's important here that participants let themselves participate even if they feel silly. Request that they humor you for a few minutes and save any evaluations until after the entire activity is completed. Assure them that if they do that, they will enhance its value.

8. Ask participants to stand with their eyes closed, holding their arms out again. Tell them to visualize that they are turning to the point at which they stopped the last time. Now ask them to visualize going 20 percent farther. Remind them that they are only doing this in their minds.

9. Tell them to return to the starting position in their minds. Now have them repeat the process in their minds, but to go 30 percent farther than their original stopping points.

10. Repeat the instructions, having them visualize going 50 percent past their original stopping places.

11. Wait a few minutes before asking participants to open their eyes. Now tell them to take their original positions, again sighting down their arms and again rotating as far as they can to the right.

12. At this point, the majority of the group will be amazed at how far they exceeded their original stopping points.

13. Conduct a debriefing session using the following questions:

    • What does this visualization suggest to you?

    • Why do you think you were able to exceed your original results?

    • Can you think of some examples of how you might use this visualization activity in your daily lives?

    • In what ways does this experience parallel your current work environment?

    • What insights can you take back to your day-to-day job environment?

QUOTE

"If you're working in a company that is not ENTHUSIASTIC, energetic, creative, clever, curious, and just plain fun, you've got troubles—serious troubles."

Tom Peters

APPENDIX

FORM C2.1

EXPERIENTIAL CONTRACT

Facilitator:

I promise to instruct this group in a safe and organized experiential education session. I promise to teach the base components of each initiative and to assist each participant in successfully learning and accomplishing each activity to the best of my ability. I promise to teach with the basic premise of "Challenge by Choice."

_____

Participant:

I promise to be open to new ideas, to offer my suggestions and to listen to those of others in the group, and to participate as fully as I can.

_____

Safety:

We agree to put safety first with all initiatives. We also agree to check with the facilitator before attempting anything that could be a safety issue.

FORM C2.2

DEBRIEFING CONTRACT

1. Honor confidentiality. Each person can control whether the conversation continues through personal input.

2. Use "I" statements, and let each statement stand on its own. Remember that you are the expert for your experience, and I am the expert for my experience.

3. Speak the truth, listen for understanding, try silence between comments, repeat what you think you heard, and ask if that is what was really meant.

4. Practice unconditional respect for self and others. Always maintain team members' self-esteem.

5. You control your own level of disclosure and involvement.

FORM C3.1

TEAM-BUILDING INTERVENTION WORKSHEET

Scheduled Intervention Date:

Location:

Facilitator(s):

Time Allotted:

Type of Team:

Team Size:

Sections
A. Team Need(s): (issues preventing team synergy)

B. Team Objective(s):

C. Recommended Facilitator Intervention(s):

D. Initiative(s):   Objective(s):   Metaphor(s)/Symbolism/
Processing Issue(s):

1   →   →

2   →   →

3   →   →

4   →   →

5   →   →

E. Safety Consideration(s):

F. Team Member(s) Issue(s): (name & issue of team member)

G. Materials Required:

1	6
2	7
3	8
4	9
5	10

FORM C3.2

LEARNING EXPERIENCE EVALUATION

Lead Facilitator:

Assistant Facilitator:

Session: Date:

1. To what extent did these activities improve team members' relationships?

   Little   1   2   3   4   5   Much

Comment:

2. To what extent do you think these activities will improve your team's communication in the future?

   Little   1   2   3   4   5   Much

Comment:

3. To what extent did these initiatives highlight the importance of collaborative team behavior?

   Little   1   2   3   4   5   Much

Comment:

4. To what extent did the facilitator provide a safe environment for the initiatives?

Little   1   2   3   4   5   Much

Comment:

5. What value would you put on these initiatives as learning tools?

Little   1   2   3   4   5   Much

Comment:

6. To what extent do you feel an increase in trust and consideration for your team-mates?

Little   1   2   3   4   5   Much

Comment:

7. To what extent would you recommend these activities to others?

Little   1   2   3   4   5   Much

Comment:

8. How effective did you find the facilitator's style?

Little   1   2   3   4   5   Very

Comment:

9. List the most effective aspects of the facilitator's style.

10. What changes would you recommend for using the initiative in the future?

50 Ways to Train Your Learner

Form C3.3

FACILITATOR'S DEBRIEFING NOTES

Date:

Group:

Lead Facilitator:

Assistant Facilitator:

_____

What Went Well:

What Could Have Been Better:

Special Issues: (Items that need to be discussed by facilitators)

Action Needed:

FORM C3.4

FOLLOW-UP SURVEY

Title of Session:

Date of Session:

It has been roughly 4 weeks since you participated in the session above. At this time, we would like to determine how what you have learned has translated back to your daily work activities. Please do not write your name on this worksheet or identify yourself in any way.

Directions: Please rate each of the following statements on a scale of 1 to 5. If you select scores at either extreme, "1" or "5," please explain why in the space provided below each question.

1. As a result of my experience, I feel more comfortable working with my fellow employees.

Strongly Disagree	Uncertain or Neutral			Strongly Agree
1	2	3	4	5

Please explain:

2. Our team has had improved communication since the initiative.

Strongly Disagree	Uncertain or Neutral			Strongly Agree
1	2	3	4	5

Please explain:

3. We were able to discover some of the collaborative behaviors that make effective teamwork possible.

      Strongly Disagree   Uncertain or Neutral   Strongly Agree
             1   2   3   4   5

Please explain:

4. I felt completely safe during the activities and would feel comfortable trying new initiatives in the future.

      Strongly Disagree   Uncertain or Neutral   Strongly Agree
             1   2   3   4   5

Please explain:

5. I feel like we were able to elevate our level of trust and consideration for one another.

      Strongly Disagree   Uncertain or Neutral   Strongly Agree
             1   2   3   4   5

Please explain:

6. The activities were useful for uncovering some of the dynamic behaviors that comprise teamwork.

      Strongly Disagree   Uncertain or Neutral   Strongly Agree
             1   2   3   4   5

Please explain:

For each statement below, circle the one ending that most closely matches your opinion.

7. Overall, this team-building initiative was:
   - Well worth the effort.
   - Probably helpful to some people.
   - Fun while it lasted.
   - A complete waste of time.

Please explain:

8. In the future, this sort of activity should be:
   - Longer.
   - Shorter.
   - About the same length of time.

Please explain:

9. The role played by the facilitator(s) in the learning experience was:
   - Very effective for my learning experience.
   - More useful in some parts than in others.
   - Occasionally beneficial to the process.
   - Problematic.

Please explain:

10. The debriefing process after each activity was:
   - Useful for stressing learning points.
   - Generally helpful in allowing me to organize my thoughts.
   - Occasionally useful in providing a suggestion.
   - Distracting.

Please explain:

11. The information I was able to take back with me to the workplace:
    - Was highlighted appropriately by the facilitator.
    - Occurred to me on my own.
    - Never seemed to happen for me.

Please explain:

12. Learning in this type of training environment probably occurs best through:
    - What we actually accomplished during the activity.
    - The experiences we shared during the debriefing.
    - Observations made by the facilitator(s).
    - The events as I perceived them on my own.
    - All of the above.

Please explain: